United States Government Accountability Office

Report to Congressional Requesters

I0448397

February 2013

SUB-SAHARAN AFRICA

Case Studies of U.S and Chinese Economic Engagement in Angola, Ghana, and Kenya; a Supplement to GAO-13-199

GAO
Accountability ★ Integrity ★ Reliability

Contents

Abbreviations

AGOA	African Growth and Opportunity Act
BEA	Bureau of Economic Analysis
Commerce	Department of Commerce
GSP	Generalized System of Preferences
IMF	International Monetary Fund
MCC	Millennium Challenge Corporation
NGO	nongovernmental organization
OECD	Organization for Economic Cooperation and Development
OPIC	Overseas Private Investment Corporation
UN	United Nations
USAID	U.S. Agency for International Development
U.S. Ex-Im	Export-Import Bank of the United States

United States Government Accountability Office
Washington, DC 20548

February 7, 2013

The Honorable James M. Inhofe
United States Senate

The Honorable Jack Kingston
House of Representatives

This supplemental report is a companion to *Sub-Saharan Africa: Trends in U.S. and Chinese Economic Engagement* (GAO-13-199).[1] This supplement presents the results of our case studies of U.S. and Chinese economic engagement in three sub-Saharan African countries— Angola, Ghana, and Kenya.[2] We conducted these case studies to compare the United States' and China's trade, grants and loans, and investment activities in sub-Saharan Africa. For contextual information about the three countries and additional information on U.S. and Chinese engagement in sub-Saharan Africa broadly, see GAO-13-199.

We selected the three countries on the basis of our assessment of the levels, types, and intersection of the United States' and China's engagement in trade, grants and loans, and investment activity in each country; the three countries' geographic diversity; and input from U.S. government officials and relevant experts. The case studies are meant to be illustrative and are not generalizable. We conducted work in Washington, D.C., and in Angola, Ghana, and Kenya, including meetings with officials from U.S. agencies, host-government ministries, U.S. businesses, other donors, and nongovernmental organizations (NGO). We were unable to meet with Chinese government officials, despite our requests, in Africa or Washington, D.C. We have noted data limitations as

---

[1] This supplemental report was prepared in conjunction with GAO-13-199, in response to a request from Representative Jack Kingston and Senator James Inhofe—then Ranking Member, Senate Foreign Relations Subcommittee on East Asian and Pacific Affairs—to review U.S. and Chinese engagement in sub-Saharan Africa.

[2] We generally report data from 2001 through 2010 or 2011, but used data for shorter periods in some cases due to data availability. For comparability, and given challenges in determining appropriate deflators for some data, we used nominal rather than inflation-adjusted values for data on trade, grants and loans, and investments. All information sources reported nominal data in U.S. dollars. All of the data we report are for calendar years, except where noted otherwise. All percentages noted in this document are rounded to the nearest number.

appropriate, such as lack of available data on China's grants and loans and likely underreporting of its investment data. Overall, we determined that the data presented in these case studies are generally reliable for the purposes for which the data are used. For a more detailed discussion of our scope and methodology, see GAO-13-199. We conducted this work from November 2011 to February 2013 in accordance with generally accepted government auditing standards.

If you or your staff members have any questions about this report, please contact me at (202) 512-3149 or gootnickd@gao.gov. Contact points for our Offices of Public Affairs and Congressional Relations may be found on the last page of this report. GAO staff who made key contributions to this report are listed in appendix I.

David B. Gootnick,
Director, International Affairs and Trade

Case Study of U.S. and Chinese Economic Engagement in Angola

U.S. and Chinese Trade with Angola

China's Total Trade in Goods in Angola Surpassed U.S. Trade in 2008, and Oil Imports Dominated Both

U.S. and Chinese trade in goods with Angola has risen dramatically, dominated by oil imports, with China's trade surpassing the United States'.[1] From 2001 through 2011, China's and the United States' total trade with Angola rose rapidly, reflecting a similarly rapid increase in imports of crude oil; China's total trade surpassed the United States' in 2008, and China's imports of crude oil exceeded the United States' in 2004 and in 2007 through 2011 (see fig. 1). Imports accounted for 90 percent of the United States' total trade with Angola, and crude oil made up 96 percent of those imports. Imports represented 90 percent of China's total trade, and almost all of its imports were crude oil.[2]

---

[1]According to the U.S. Department of Energy, Angola has been a large oil producer for decades and is a member of the Organization of Petroleum Exporting Countries.

[2]In addition to importing crude oil, both countries have imported diamonds since 2003; in 2011, the United States imported $169 million in diamonds and China imported $99 million in diamonds. The United States also imported $510 million in noncrude oil (which includes refined oil) in 2011, whereas China imported none. As in 2011, crude and noncrude oil were the top imports for the United States and crude oil was the top import for China in 2001.

Figure 1: U.S. and Chinese Total Trade in Goods with Angola, Including Crude Oil Imports, 2001-2011

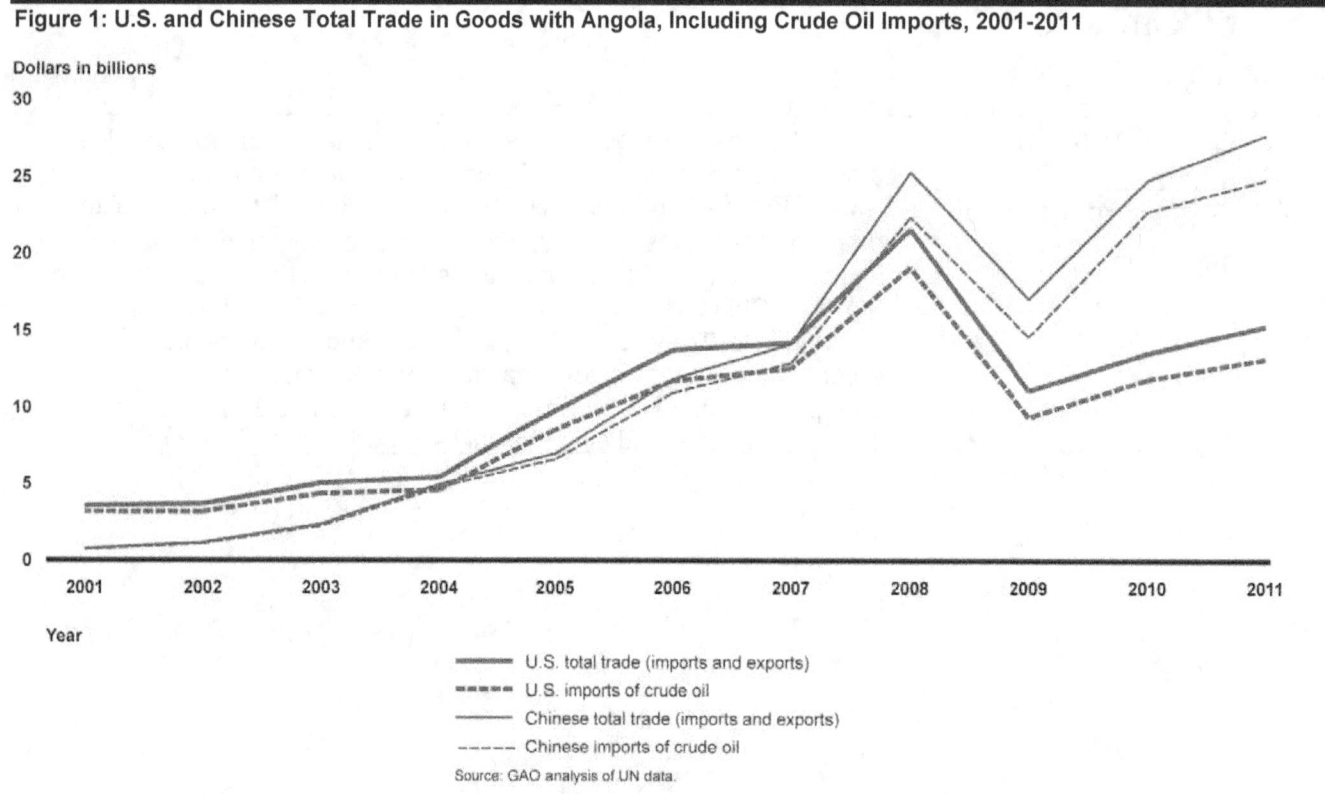

Dollars in billions

Year

U.S. total trade (imports and exports)

U.S. imports of crude oil

Chinese total trade (imports and exports)

Chinese imports of crude oil

Source: GAO analysis of UN data.

Notes: Total trade is defined as imports plus exports. Trade data are reported in nominal values. Changes in value over time are due in part to changes in the prices of traded goods, such as substantial increases in the price of oil.

Almost all of U.S. imports from Angola enter the United States without tariffs. Since 2004, after Angola became eligible as a beneficiary of the African Growth and Opportunity Act (AGOA), the U.S. trade-preference program, 52 percent of total U.S. imports, including 53 percent of U.S. oil imports, from Angola have been tariff free under the program's terms. In addition, since 2001, 42 percent of total U.S. imports from Angola, including 43 percent of U.S. oil imports from Angola, have been tariff free under the Generalized System of Preferences (GSP). All imports from Angola under AGOA have consisted of oil, primarily crude oil. Figure 2 shows U.S. imports under AGOA from Angola from 2004 through 2011.

Figure 2: U.S. Imports of Goods under AGOA from Angola, 2004-2011

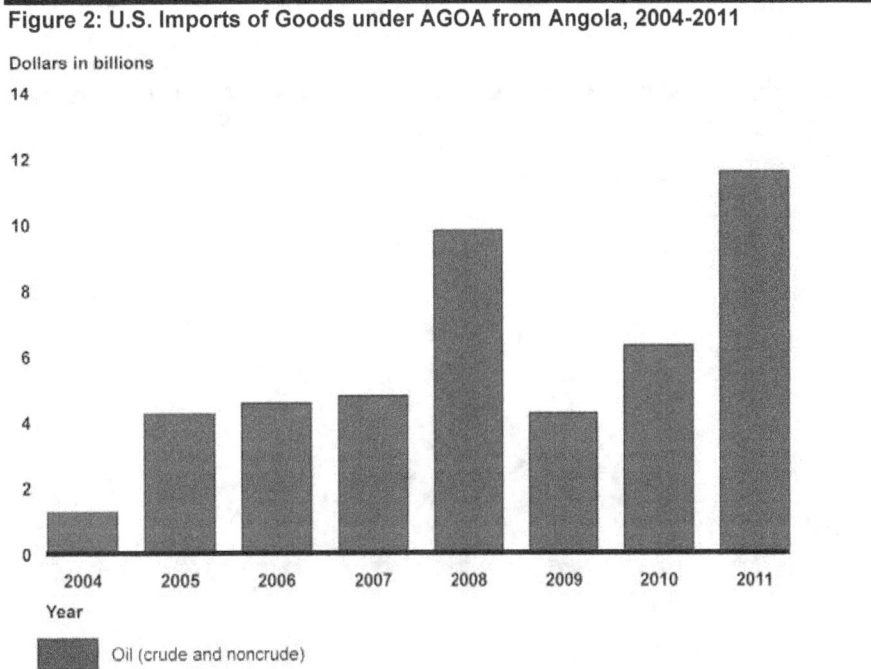

Dollars in billions

Oil (crude and noncrude)

Source: GAO analysis of Department of Commerce data.

Notes: All U.S. imports under AGOA from Angola during this period consisted of oil. Angola became elig ble to export goods under AGOA in 2004. Data are shown in nominal values.

Almost all Chinese imports from least developed countries, which include Angola, enter China without tariffs. In 2003, China announced that some commodities from least developed countries in Africa, which includes Angola, would be given duty-free status. By 2007, according to a report by the World Trade Organization that cited Chinese officials, 98 percent of the total value of Chinese imports from least developed countries, which include Angola, entered China tariff free.

Like its imports, China's exports to Angola exceed U.S. exports. In 2011, China exported just under $2.8 billion in goods to Angola, while the United States exported less than $1.5 billion. Although China exported relatively few goods to Angola in 2001, its exports rapidly increased and surpassed those of the United States in 2008. In 2011, top Chinese exports included manufactured goods (e.g., cement, iron and steel rails) and machinery and transport equipment (e.g., electric generators and motorcycles). Top U.S. exports to Angola included machinery and transport equipment such as civil-engineering equipment, and food such as frozen poultry products. Figure 3 shows the trends and composition of U.S. and Chinese exports to Angola from 2001 through 2011.

Figure 3: U.S. and Chinese Exports of Goods to Angola, 2001-2011

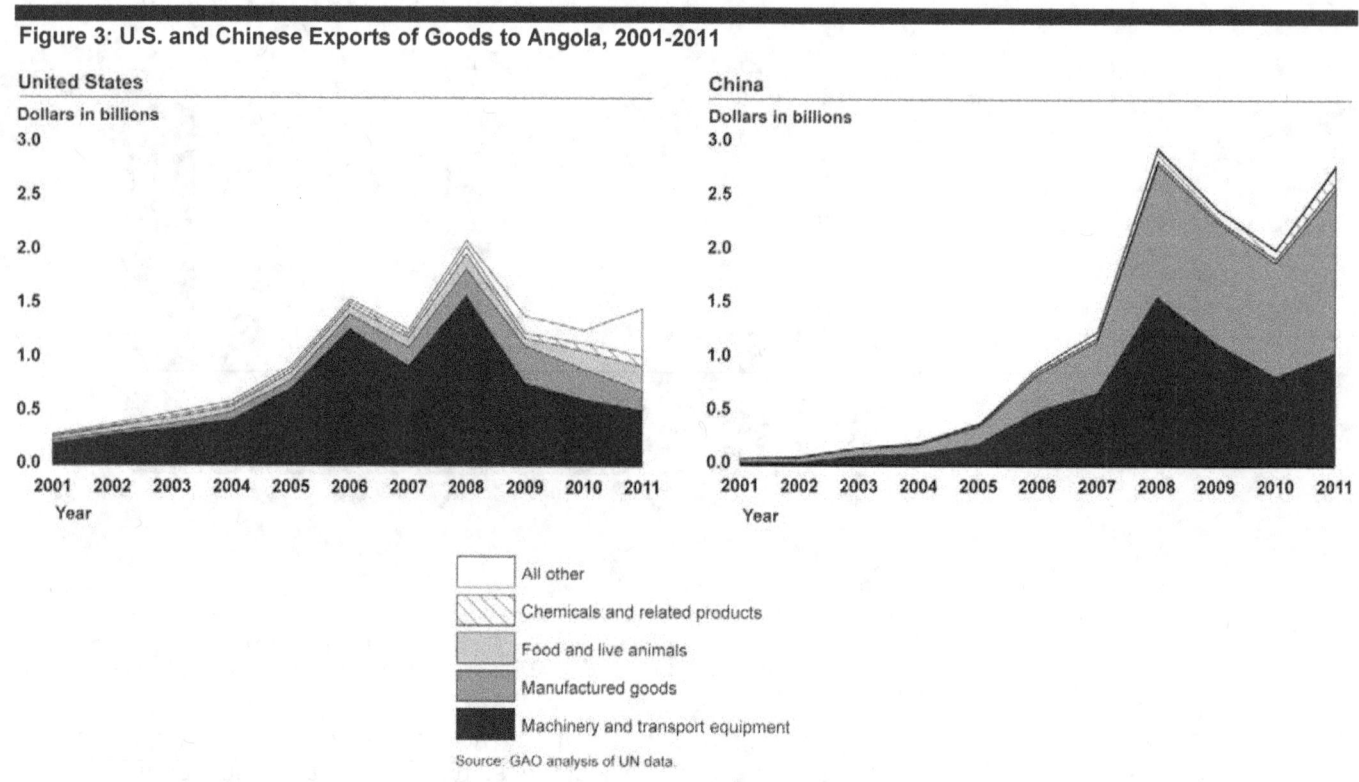

Source: GAO analysis of UN data.

Note: Export data are reported in nominal dollars.

U.S. Trade in Services with Angola Is Estimated at About $2.4 Billion per Year, but No Comparable Data Are Available for China's Trade in Services	From 2006 through 2011, total U.S. trade in services with Angola averaged about $2.2 billion annually, with U.S. imports of services averaging about $411 million and U.S. exports of services averaging about $1.8 billion.[3] For U.S. trade in services with Angola, the largest sectors for U.S. imports were transportation services and travel and passenger fares, and the largest sector for exports was business, professional, and technical services.[4] No comparable data are available for China's trade in services with Angola, in part because China does not publish country-specific information on its trade in services.
U.S. Firms Generally Have Not Competed with Chinese Firms on World Bank–Financed and Host-Government Contracts	U.S. and Chinese firms largely have not competed in similar sectors in Angola for donor-funded and host-government contracts, including contracts for provision of goods and services. According to data on World Bank-financed contracts in Angola for which U.S. and Chinese firms won contracts between 2001 and 2011, Chinese firms won fewer contracts but a larger share of contract dollars than U.S. firms and were active in providing construction services.[5] U.S. firms won a smaller share of contract dollars and were primarily active in consulting services, such as management and technical advice, and legal advisory services. Figure 4 shows World Bank contracts in Angola that firms from the United States, China, and other countries won in 2001 through 2011.

---

[3]To calculate estimates of total trade in services, including imports and exports of services, we used the higher value when ranges of estimates were provided for sectors of services such as business, professional, and technical services. Therefore, the averages we report represent the higher end of values in underlying tabulations from the Bureau of Economic Analysis (BEA) and other sources and our analysis of BEA's survey data.

[4]From 2006 through 2011, annual U.S. imports averaged $212 million for transportation services and $98 million for travel and passenger fares. From 2009 through 2011 annual U.S. exports averaged approximately $1 billion to $1.5 billion annually for business, professional, and technical services.

[5]Services provided by U.S. firms under World Bank–funded contracts represent a small fraction (less than 1 percent) of annual U.S. trade in service exports to Angola. However, World Bank contracts represent one of the few instances where data are available for examination of potential competition between U.S. and Chinese firms. According to the World Bank, the data include only contracts reviewed by World Bank staff prior to award, which constitute about 40 percent of total World Bank investment lending. The nationality of a firm reflects the country where it is registered, although the firm's parent may be headquartered in another country.

Figure 4: World Bank-Financed Contracts Won by Firms from the United States, China, and Other Countries in Angola, 2001-2011

Firm's country of origin	Number of contracts	World Bank contract dollars won, percentage	Contract value by categories, dollars in millions	Top three contract types, number of contracts
United States	7	⌐ 2	⌐ $1 ▼ $4	Management/technical advice .... 4 Equipment, information technology .... 1 Legal advisory services 1
China	3	17	$39	Construction services, maintenance .... 2 and rehabilitation Construction services, building 1
Other countries[a]	342	81	$84　　$76　$21	Management/technical advice .... 105 Project management .... 43 Procurement technical assistance 19

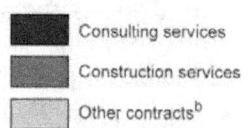

■ Consulting services

▬ Construction services

□ Other contracts[b]

Source: GAO analysis of World Bank data.

Notes: According to the World Bank, the data shown include only contracts reviewed by World Bank staff prior to award. In general, these types of contracts constitute about 40 percent of total World Bank investment lending. The nationality of a firm reflects the country in which it is registered, although the firm's parent may be headquartered in another country.

[a]Firms from at least 26 other countries won World Bank contracts, with Angolan and Portuguese firms winning the most contracts.

[b]Other contracts were primarily for goods such as transportation equipment, information technology equipment, and educational equipment.

Department of Commerce (Commerce) data on U.S. firms bidding on host-government contracts provide some evidence that U.S. firms primarily competed with European firms for these contracts. From August 2002 to February 2012, U.S. firms requested assistance from Commerce's Advocacy Center in competing for eight Angolan government contracts for goods and services. French, British, and Italian firms competed with U.S. firms for more of these contracts and in more sectors—primarily the oil and gas sector and the energy and power sector—than did Chinese firms (see fig. 5). Chinese firms competed for only one of the contracts, for locomotives in the transportation sector.

Figure 5: Nationality of Firms Competing for Eight Angolan Government Contracts for Goods and Services, 2002- 2012

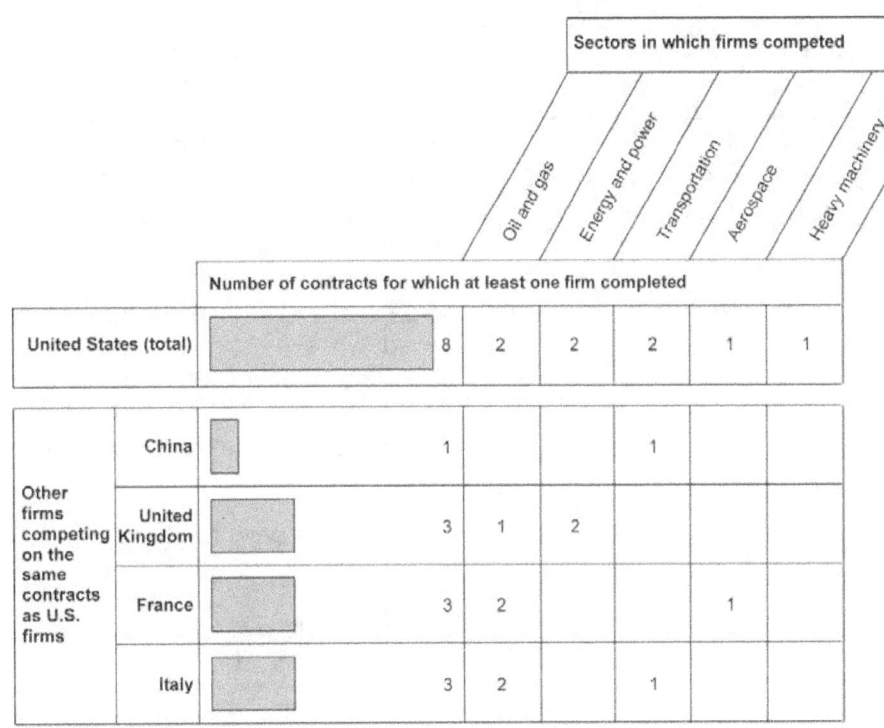

		Number of contracts for which at least one firm completed	Oil and gas	Energy and power	Transportation	Aerospace	Heavy machinery
United States (total)		8	2	2	2	1	1
Other firms competing on the same contracts as U.S. firms	China	1		1			
	United Kingdom	3	1	2			
	France	3	2			1	
	Italy	3	2		1		

Source: GAO analysis of Department of Commerce data.

Notes: Data shown are for eight Angolan government contracts for which U.S. firms requested Commerce advocacy assistance in August 2002 through February 2012. Firms from the United Kingdom, France, and Italy competed with U.S firms for the largest numbers of contracts.

U.S. and Chinese Grants and Loans to Angola

U.S. Government Committed About $800 Million in Grants to Angola, but Data Are Not Available for China's Grants

From 2001 to 2010, the U.S. government committed $804 million in grants to Angola,[6] primarily for health and humanitarian assistance.[7] As figure 6 shows, the level of U.S. government aid to Angola has varied over time, peaking in 2003 at about $152 million, declining until 2006 as humanitarian assistance was reduced sharply, and increasing again somewhat by 2010. The composition of U.S. aid to Angola has also varied over time, with humanitarian assistance constituting the bulk of assistance between 2002 and 2005 and health assistance generally increasing from 2006 to 2010. In contrast to the United States, China does not publish data on its grants to Angola.

---

[6]According to USAID officials, the U.S. government committed almost all of its grants to organizations operating in Angola, not to the government of Angola.

[7]U.S. development assistance data for 2011 were not available at the time of this report's publication.

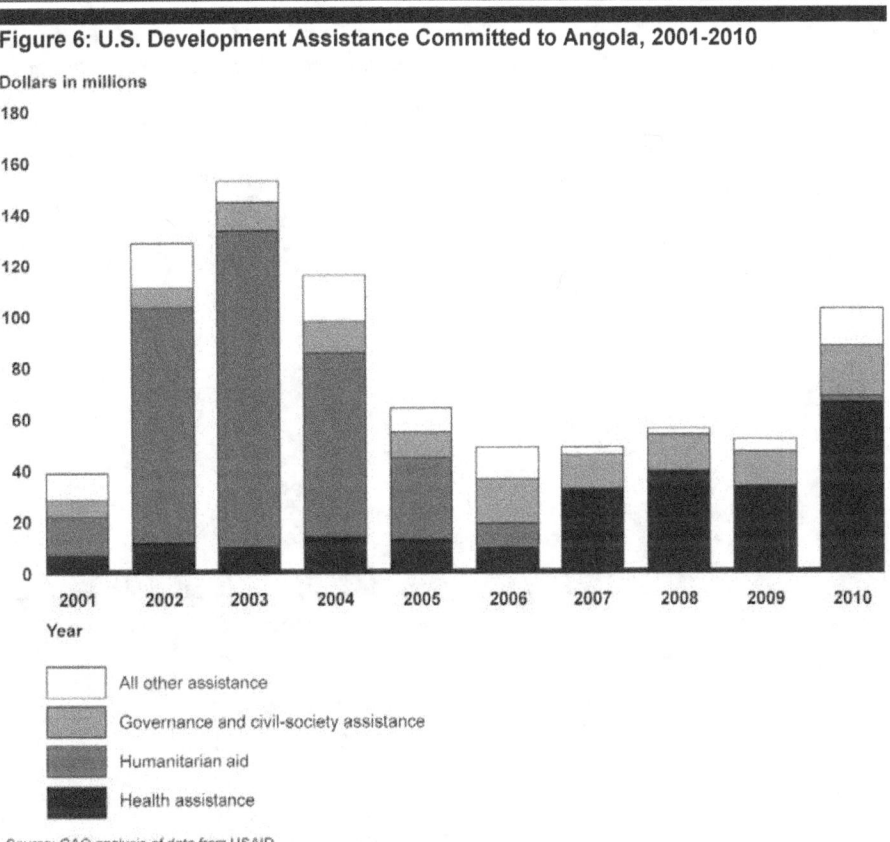

Figure 6: U.S. Development Assistance Committed to Angola, 2001-2010

Dollars in millions

Year

All other assistance

Governance and civil-society assistance

Humanitarian aid

Health assistance

Source: GAO analysis of data from USAID.

Note: Aid data are shown in nominal dollars by calendar year.

Chinese Government Loan Commitments to Angola Significantly Exceed U.S. Government Loan Commitments for Trade and Investment

The U.S. government committed about $711 million in loans and related financing, such as loan guarantees and insurance, between 2001 through 2011 to support U.S. exports to, and U.S. firms' investments in, Angola. The Export-Import Bank of the United States (U.S. Ex-Im) committed about $678 million—95 percent of total U.S. government loan commitments— primarily for U.S. aerospace products and parts. Also, through OPIC, the U.S. government committed about $32 million in financing from 2001 through 2011 to support U.S. firms' investments in Angola in sectors such as credit financing, cement and concrete manufacturing, and grain and oilseed milling. Figure 7 shows U.S. government loans and related financing committed for U.S.-made products and U.S. firms' investments in Angola from 2001 through 2011.

Figure 7: U.S. Government Loans and Related Financing Committed for U.S.-Made Products and U.S. Firms' Investments in Angola, 2001-2011

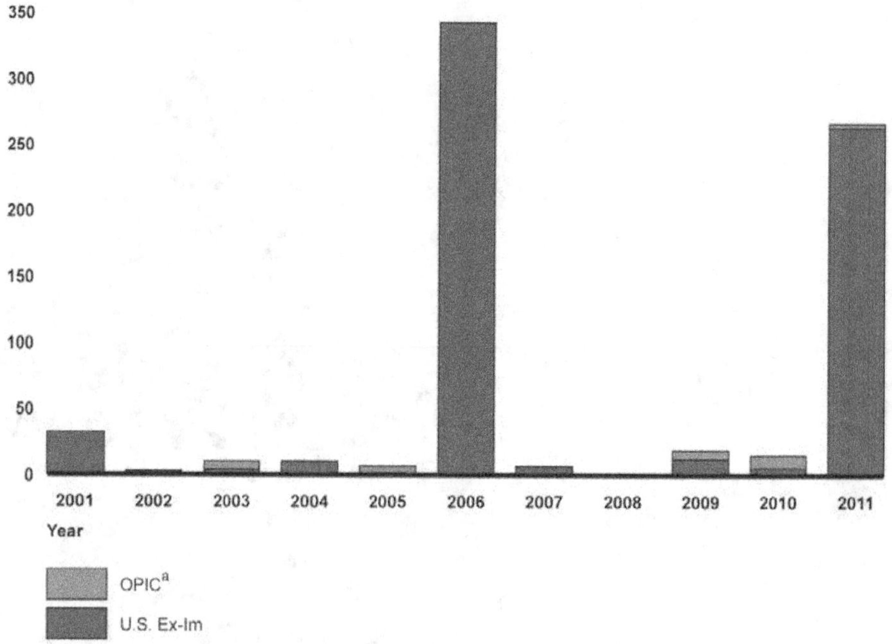

Dollars in millions

Source: GAO analysis of data from U.S. Ex-Im and OPIC.

Notes: Data are shown in nominal dollars. In addition, these values are shown by calendar year, although U.S. Ex-Im and OPIC typically report data by fiscal year.

[a]OPIC may report data for some financing commitments, such as investment funds, only at the regional level. Data shown do not reflect OPIC investment funds for regional use in sub-Saharan Africa, possibly including Angola. According to OPIC officials, because recipients of OPIC investment assistance may choose to invest in a set of countries, OPIC may initially lack information such as the countries where investments are made. In addition, according to OPIC officials, in countries with limited investment activity, business confidentiality agreements may prevent the disclosure of data that would reveal details of individual transactions.

As of September 2012, the Chinese government had committed an estimated $12 billion in credit lines to Angola since 2002 through the Export-Import Bank of China and the China Development Bank (see table

1),[8] according to the Angolan Ministry of Finance and a U.S. official.[9] Chinese government loans to Angola are generally guaranteed by Angola's oil in case of default and are repaid through proceeds from the sale of oil, according to officials from the U.S. government and a donor agency in Angola. According to the Angolan Ministry of Finance, U.S. officials, and a donor agency official in Angola, Chinese government loans to Angola have been for infrastructure construction, such as roads, rail, hospitals, schools, housing, water supply, and telecommunications.

Table 1: Chinese Credit Lines to Angola since 2002

Dollars in billions

Year committed	Financing committed	Types of projects
2004	$2.0	Roads, rail, airports, housing, water supply, hospitals, schools, telecommunications, boats
2007	2.5	
2009	7.5	
Total	**$12.0**	

Source: GAO analysis of information from the Angolan Ministry of Finance, U.S. officials, and a donor agency official in Angola.

Note: Data shown are those available as of September 2012.

A large number of Chinese laborers work in Angola on projects financed by the Chinese government and implemented by Chinese firms.[10] As part of their loan agreement, the governments of China and Angola agreed that 70 percent of workers implementing construction projects would be Chinese and the remaining 30 percent would be Angolans, according to an Angolan nongovernmental organization (NGO) and reported statements by the former Chinese ambassador to Angola.[11] However, the

---

[8]A credit line represents funding available to a borrower, who incurs a loan by drawing funds from the credit line. Comprehensive information on disbursement of China's credit lines and loans to Angola is not available. However, data published by the Angolan Ministry of Finance indicate that as of June 2008, about 30 percent of China's credit lines of $2 billion in 2004 and $2.5 billion in 2007 had been disbursed. Additionally, according to a U.S. official, data from Angolan Ministry of Finance indicate that as of September 2010, Angola owed China about $3 billion.

[9]China's total lending and some additional information about the loans to Angola is corroborated by other sources.

[10] Brazilian and Portuguese firms are also constructing infrastructure in Angola, according to an official from an Angolan firm, an Angolan NGO, and a U.S. official.

[11]According to an Angolan NGO, Chinese-made materials must also constitute 70 percent of the materials used for these construction projects.

Angolan NGO and former Chinese ambassador noted that Chinese firms usually did not meet Angola's requirements for local hiring; according to the Angolan NGO, this resulted in part from a lack of skills among Angolans after the country's long civil war.[12] Consequently, a large number of Chinese work in Angola on these projects.[13] For example, data published by China's Ministry of Commerce showed that more than 31,000 Chinese laborers were in Angola by 2009, and the former Chinese ambassador to Angola estimated that between 60,000 and 70,000 Chinese were in Angola in 2011, to implement projects financed through the Chinese credit lines, according to a news report published in March 2011. Figure 8 shows examples of Chinese firms' construction projects in Angola.

---

[12]Angola's Ministry of Finance published a list of projects that were being financed by the Export-Import Bank of China's credit lines as of the second quarter of 2008. This list includes information such as the number of Chinese and Angolan workers associated with projects but may not include all projects financed by the Export-Import Bank of China's credit lines and does not include information on the number of Chinese and Angolan workers for every project. However, in contrast to statements by an Angolan NGO and the former Chinese ambassador, the available information for the listed projects indicated that 36 percent of workers were Chinese and 64 percent were Angolans.

[13]According to a survey of Angolan workers employed at both Western (including Brazilian) and Chinese construction and oil firms, workers at Chinese firms tend to be younger, have less work experience, work longer hours per day, be less educated, and earn less compared with workers at Western firms. Worker turnover is also higher at Chinese firms.

Figure 8: Examples of Construction Projects Implemented by Chinese Firms in Angola

Source: GAO.

Left to right: Signage for a Chinese firm constructing a building in downtown Luanda, Angola. Housing units near Luanda, Angola, being constructed by Chinese firms, according to a U.S. official.

The Chinese government's engagement with Angola has been evolving since 2002. According to an expert in China-Africa relations, the Chinese government was one of the first foreign governments to provide relatively cheap financing to Angola after the country's civil war ended in 2002. According to an Angolan NGO, China provided this financing without significant conditions and, partly as a result of this financing, has developed relatively close ties with the Angolan government. After the end of Angola's civil war, the Angolan government emphasized rapid reconstruction, according to an Angolan NGO and officials from U.S. and Angolan firms.[14] However, according to Angolan government officials, the government is now focused on reducing poverty and diversifying the economy.

---

[14]According to Angolan NGOs and an official from an Angolan firm, during the initial stages of Angola's reconstruction, Chinese contractors received little supervision. Inadequate supervision contributed to low quality of Chinese construction, according to Angolan NGOs and donor agency officials.

U.S. and Chinese Investments in Angola

U.S. firms' investments in Angola, largely in the oil sector, exceed Chinese firms' reported investments. U.S. cumulative foreign direct investment flows from 2007 through 2011 were $3.4 billion,[15] while China's reported investment flows were about $214 million (see fig. 9). According to experts, data on China's foreign direct investments are likely under-reported,[16] and according to the Bureau of Economic Analysis (BEA), data on U.S. foreign direct investments may also be underreported,[17] limiting precise comparisons of the United States' and China's investments. BEA reports that in 2011, the top sector of U.S. foreign direct investment stock was mining, predominantly crude-oil extraction, and that from 2006 through 2011, one of the fastest growing sectors was companies related to oil-related manufacturing. Comparable data for China's foreign direct investment in Angola by sector are not available.

[15]According to the Organization for Economic Cooperation and Development (OECD), foreign direct investment is the ownership by a foreign person or business of 10 percent or more of the voting equity of a firm located in the host country. Foreign direct investment flows provide information for foreign direct investment activity within a given *period* of time, while foreign direct investment stock indicates the level of foreign direct investment at a given *point* in time. U.S. foreign direct investment flows during 2007 through 2011 were volatile, with a negative flow in 2007 and a spike in 2010.

[16]According to experts, Chinese firms set up subsidiaries, in places such as Hong Kong and the British Virgin Islands, that can be used to make investments in sub-Saharan Africa. Such investments are not captured by China's data on foreign direct investment and may be a significant source of underreporting. In addition, many small and medium-sized enterprises may not register their foreign direct investments, which therefore may not be reflected in China's data. According to an International Monetary Fund (IMF) working paper, China's foreign direct investment data also show inconsistencies between investment flows and changes in investment stock that are difficult to explain (see Montfort Mlachila and Misa Takebe, "FDI from BRICs to LICs: Emerging Growth Driver?" *IMF Working* Paper, WP/11/178 [2011], 11). Finally, China does not define foreign direct investment when reporting its data. However, the types of data that China reports for its foreign direct investments (e.g., equity investment data, reinvested earnings data) are similar to data reported for U.S. foreign direct investment. Moreover, China's reported foreign direct investment data represent official information published by the Chinese government and, despite their limitations, have been used in various reports, including those published by international organizations (e.g., the IMF), government agencies, academic experts, and other research institutions, to describe China's foreign direct investment activities in Africa.

[17]BEA noted that these data may not include investments in Sub-Saharan Africa by U.S. firms through subsidiaries in locations such as the Netherlands. According to BEA, U.S. foreign direct investment data are based on a 2009 benchmark survey that covers the value of all U.S. foreign direct investment, but these data may not reflect foreign direct investments by smaller firms.

Figure 9: Reported Flows of Foreign Direct Investment from the United States and China to Angola, 2007-2011

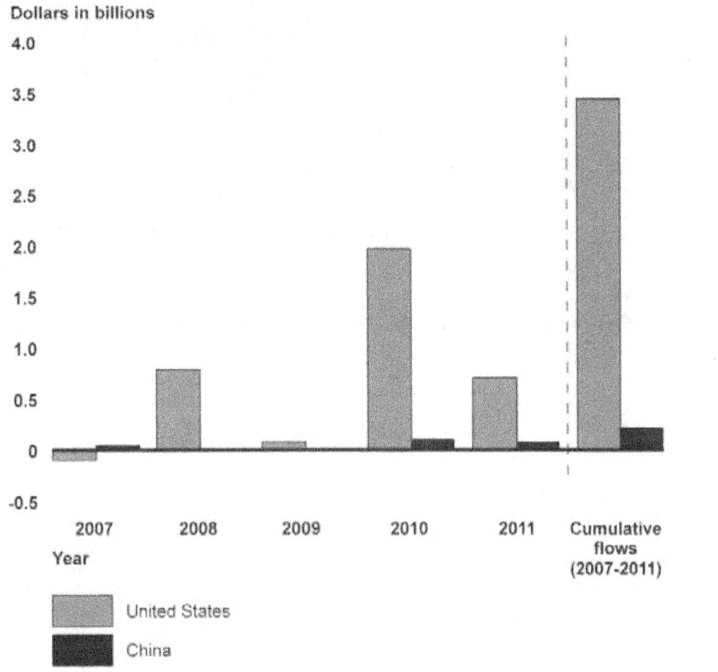

Dollars in billions

Source: GAO analysis of data from BEA, China's Ministry of Commerce, China's National Bureau of Statistics, and Haver Analytics.

Note: Data are shown in nominal values.

Data on the purchase of ownership interests in oil blocks in Angola indicate that as of September 2012, U.S. firms were active in Angola's petroleum sector (see fig. 10).[18] No single foreign firm dominates Angola's oil sector, because the Angolan government tends to distribute ownership stake among multiple companies. However, U.S. firms act as operators for 11 of 49 oil blocks and have primary responsibility for operations such as drilling, maintenance, and complying with required

---

[18]An oil block is a geographic area delineated by the licensing authorities for oil exploration and production. The licensing authority grants exploration and/or production rights to the oil company or joint venture within the boundaries of the block, usually on an exclusive basis.

rules and regulations.[19] In addition, U.S. firms have purchased ownership interests in 5 oil blocks as nonoperators, generally with a minority stake but no responsibility for operations. Chinese firms, generally lacking the technology and capacity to manage offshore oil operations, have purchased ownership interests as nonoperators in 12 oil blocks in Angola.[20] Like other nonoperators, Chinese firms' ownership interests help mitigate the operator's financial risks, given the large investments required in oil exploration and production operations. In addition, through these ownership interests, Chinese firms participate in, and learn management experience through, the decision-making process of oil well operations, according to an official from a major oil firm.

Figure 10: Numbers and Types of U.S. and Chinese Firms' Investments in Oil Blocks in Angola as of September 2012

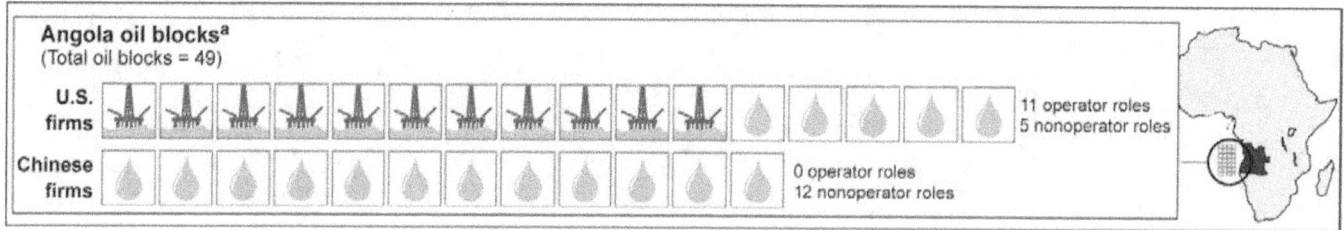

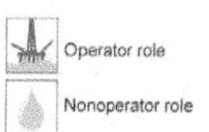

Source: GAO analysis of data from the U.S. Department of Energy and the government of Angola (data); MapInfo (map).

[a]In addition to U.S. firms, firms from Angola, Brazil, Denmark, France, and the United Kingdom, among others, operate Angola's 49 oil blocks.

---

[19]An operator is generally the oil company that engages in drilling, service, and other operations; an operator has primary responsibility for maintaining well operations and ensuring compliance with required rules and regulations. A nonoperator generally has an ownership stake, similar to a minority and noncontrolling interest.

[20]According to the U.S. Department of Energy, Chinese firms are gaining experience managing offshore oil operations in other sub-Saharan African countries and in Asia.

Case Study of U.S. and Chinese Economic Engagement in Ghana

U.S. and Chinese Trade with Ghana

Chinese Trade in Goods Has Exceeded U.S. Trade and Grown More Rapidly

Since 2003, China's total trade in goods with Ghana has surpassed U.S. trade (see fig. 11). From 2001 through 2011, the United States' total trade with Ghana grew by a factor of 5, from approximately $384 million to nearly $2 billion, while China's total trade with Ghana grew by a factor of 19, from approximately $182 million to nearly $3.5 billion. Exports to Ghana made up a significant portion of both the United States' total trade (66 percent) and China's total trade (approximately 92 percent) during that 11-year period.

Figure 11: U.S. and Chinese Total Trade in Goods with Ghana, 2001-2011

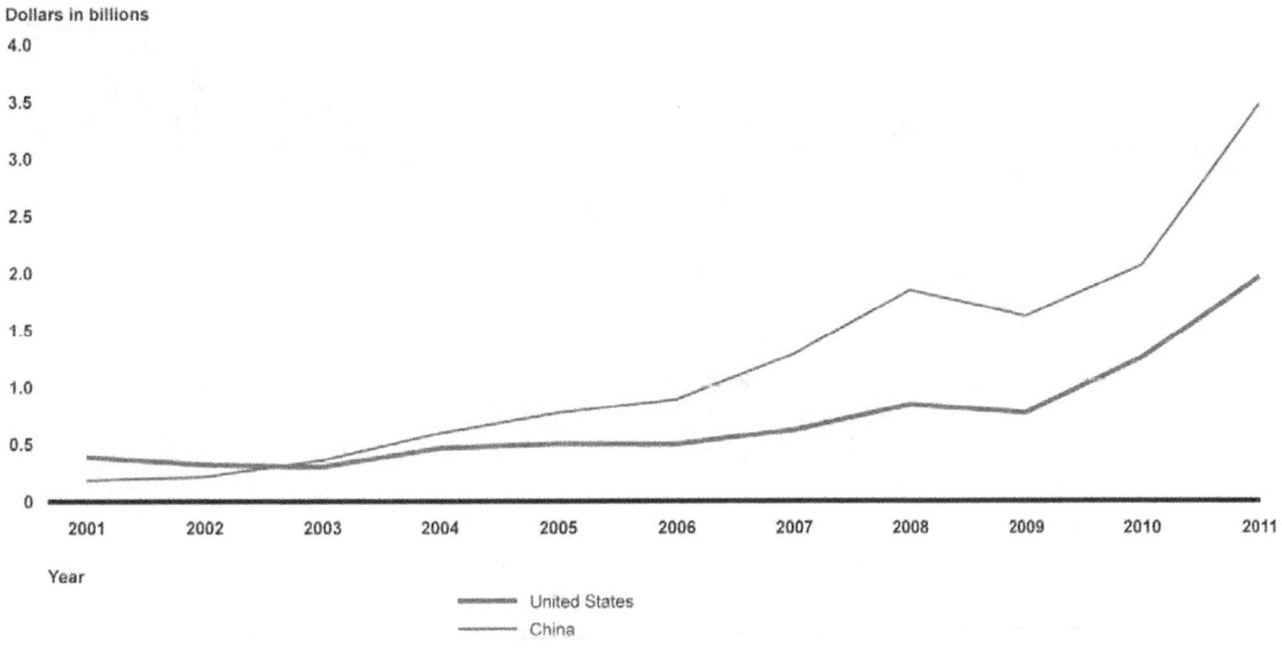

Dollars in billions

Year

United States

China

Source: GAO analysis of UN data.

Notes: Total trade is defined as imports plus exports. Trade data are reported in nominal values. Changes in value over time are due in part to changes in the prices of traded goods.

In 2001, the United States' and China's exports to Ghana were similar in value—approximately $179 million and nearly $146 million, respectively—but by 2011, Chinese exports had grown more than 20-fold, to $3.1 billion. This growth was largely due to increased exports of manufactured goods, such as footwear and lighting fixtures, and of chemicals such as insecticides. As figure 12 shows, the United States exported approximately $1.2 billion in goods to Ghana in 2011, six times its exports in 2001. Top U.S. exports in 2011 included machinery and transport equipment, mainly machinery for minerals extraction and motor vehicles, and mineral fuels, primarily refined oil. Figure 12 shows U.S. and Chinese exports to Ghana by key categories.

Figure 12: U.S. and Chinese Exports of Goods to Ghana, 2001-2011

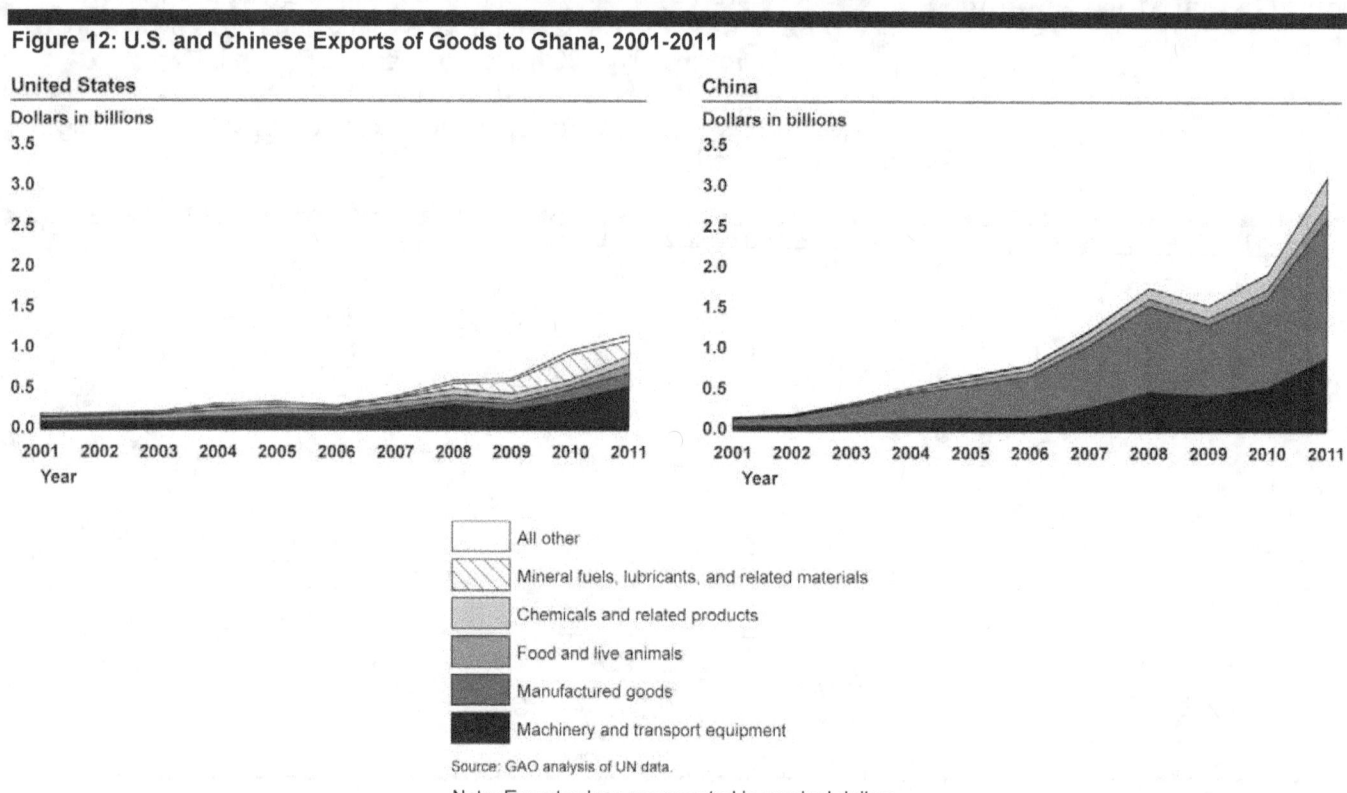

Source: GAO analysis of UN data.

Note: Export values are reported in nominal dollars.

U.S. imports of goods from Ghana have exceeded Chinese imports. U.S. imports increased nearly fourfold from 2001 to 2011, growing from approximately $200 million in 2001 to $800 million in 2011 (see fig. 13). Since 2001, the United States has increased its imports of cocoa from Ghana. Ghana became an oil-producing nation at the end of 2010 after a U.S. company discovered oil offshore in 2007, and crude oil was the top U.S. import from Ghana in 2011. However, Chinese imports from Ghana grew more rapidly than U.S. imports in the same period, rising 10-fold, from almost $37 million in 2001 to more than $360 million in 2011. China

increased its imports of ores from 2001 to 2011 and also began importing
crude oil in 2011.

Figure 13: U.S. and Chinese Imports of Goods from Ghana, 2001-2011

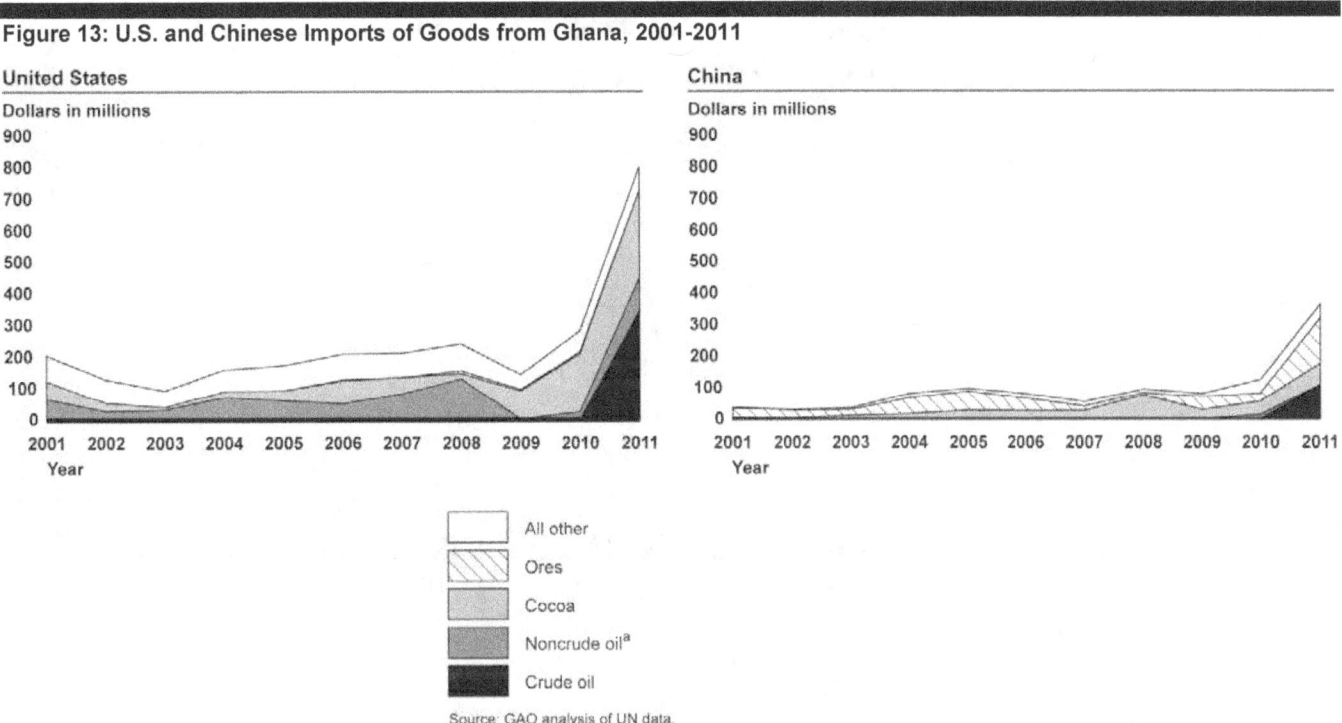

Source: GAO analysis of UN data.

Note: Data are shown in nominal dollars.

[a]Noncrude oil includes refined oil such as gasoline and kerosene.

Under AGOA, the U.S. trade preference program, oil constituted 95
percent of U.S. imports from Ghana from 2001 to 2011 (see fig. 14). U.S.
imports of oil under AGOA, mostly crude oil, grew significantly in 2011, to
nearly $413 million, compared with approximately $288 million in imports
of oil, all noncrude, for the prior 10 years. The United States imported
nearly $739 million in total goods from Ghana under AGOA during that
period, including about $36 million of textiles, apparel, leather, and
footwear, the second largest category of AGOA imports after oil.[1]
Because Ghana is not a least developed country, it does not qualify for

[1]From 2001 to 2011, tariffs on a combined total of nearly $906 million in U.S. imports
(approximately 39 percent of total U.S. imports) from Ghana were eliminated under AGOA
and GSP.

duty exemptions under China's trade preferences for least developed
countries.

Figure 14: U.S. Imports of Goods under AGOA from Ghana, 2001-2011

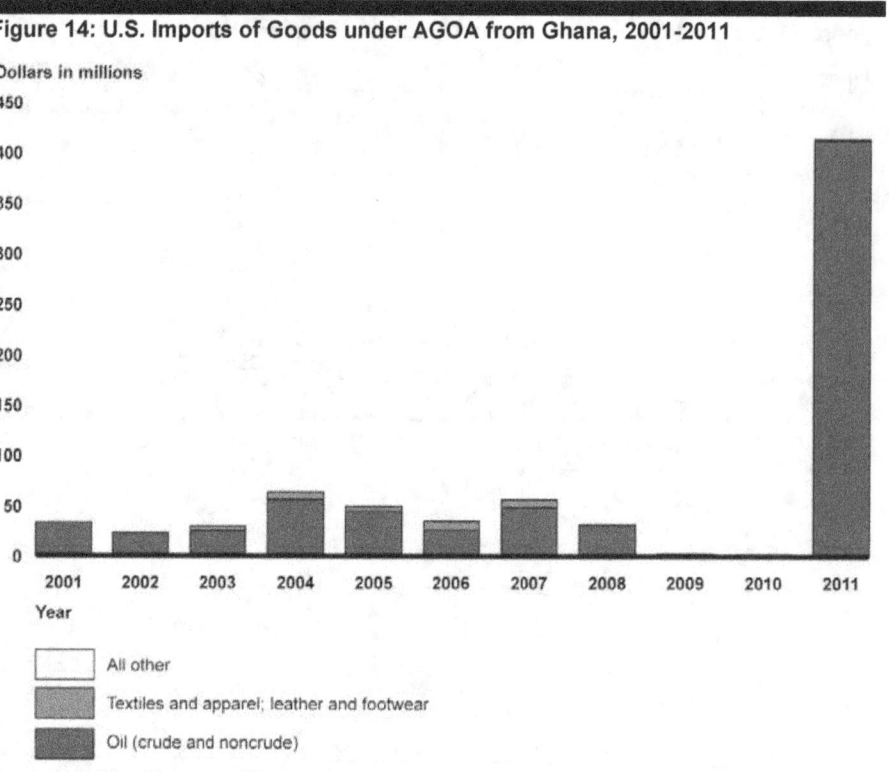

Source: GAO analysis of Department of Commerce data.

Note: Data are shown in nominal dollars. Data represented as "all other"—imports ranging from
approximately $6,000 in 2001 to approximately $2 million in 2009—are not visble because of the
magnitude of petroleum imports in 2011.

U.S. Trade in Services with Ghana Is Estimated at About $1.4 Billion per Year, but Comparable Data Are Not Available for China's Trade in Services	From 2006 to 2011, total U.S. trade in services with Ghana averaged about $1.2 billion annually, with U.S. imports of services averaging about $644 million per year and U.S. exports of services averaging about $546 million per year.[2] The largest sector for U.S. imports of services was travel and passenger fares. The largest sectors for U.S. exports of services were business, professional, and technical services; and travel and passenger fares. No comparable data are available for China's trade in services, in part because China does not publish country-specific information on its trade in services.

U.S. and Chinese Firms' Competition for Donor-Funded and Host-Government Contracts Has Been Limited

U.S. and Chinese firms generally have not competed in similar sectors in Ghana for donor-funded contracts. According to data on Millennium Challenge Corporation (MCC)–funded projects in Ghana for which U.S. and Chinese firms won contracts in 2007 through 2012, all MCC contracts implemented by Chinese firms were for construction projects. Furthermore, officials who oversaw procurement for MCC-funded contracts in Ghana said that U.S. firms did not bid on any MCC construction contracts (see table 2).

Table 2: U.S., Chinese, and Other Firms' Participation in MCC Contracts for Ghana, 2007-2012

Contractor nationality	Number of projects[a]	MCC contract dollars won, percent of final contract amounts	Contract amount, dollars in millions	Consulting services, percent of contract amount	Construction, percent of contract amount	Goods, percent of contract amount
United States	11	6%	$31.9	100%	0%	0%
China	7	22	111.7	0	100	0
Ghana	>400	37	192.2	29	54	17
Other countries	>200	35	177	28	71	2

Source: GAO analysis of Millennium Challenge Corporation data.

[2]From 2006 through 2011, annual U.S. imports averaged between $50 million to $200 million for business, professional, and technical services, $350 million for travel and passenger fares, $31 million for education services, and $3 million for transportation services. During the same period, annual U.S. exports averaged between $50 million and $200 million for business, professional, and technical services, $118 million for travel and passenger fares, $91 million for education services, and $22 million for transportation services. To calculate total trade, imports, and exports to Ghana, we used the higher value when ranges of estimates were provided for sectors of services such as business, professional, and technical services. The averages reported are the highest of possible values in underlying tabulations from BEA and other sources and our analysis of BEA's survey data.

[a]Numbers of projects shown are estimates, particularly for contractors from Ghana and other countries, owing to the size and complexity of MCC's procurement system.

Implementation of MCC's 5-year, $547 million compact with Ghana began in 2007, with a focus on reducing poverty through agribusiness development. As table 2 shows, U.S. firms won 11 MCC contracts totaling nearly $32 million (6 percent of the value of MCC contracts in Ghana), all for consulting services. Chinese firms won 7 contracts totaling approximately $112 million (22 percent of the value of MCC contracts in Ghana), nearly 40 percent of which funded construction of a section of the National "N1" Highway in Accra (see fig. 15).[3] Because of the higher values of construction contracts, Chinese firms' contracts were larger (5 of the 10 largest MCC contracts) than U.S. firms' (1 of the 10 MCC largest contracts). The majority of Chinese-implemented MCC construction projects were transportation projects; the remaining projects were agriculture-related infrastructure, such as irrigation systems.

---

[3]MCC does not favor companies by nationality in competing for contracts, and procurement guidelines specify open, fair, and competitive procedures consistent with delivering effective aid. In 2010, MCC revised its guidelines to exclude state-owned enterprises from competing for MCC-funded contracts to ensure level competition with firms that otherwise would not receive government support. At the time the regulation was put into effect, the success of Chinese state-owned enterprises in winning MCC contracts received particular attention. The regulation went into effect after a number of MCC contracts in Ghana were awarded, and MCC and Ghanaian government officials said it did not affect their work. Ghanaian firms won about $192 million in MCC contracts, 38 percent of the total amount of contracted work performed, more than half of which was for construction work. Portuguese firms won nearly $114 million in contracts, or approximately 22 percent of the total contracted work, all of which was for construction.

Figure 15: Photos of MCC-Funded N1 Highway and Signage in Ghana

Source: GAO.

Left to right: MCC-funded N1 Highway in Accra, Ghana, built in part by China Railway Wuju Corporation. MCC signage over N1 Highway.

Data on World Bank–funded contracts in Ghana also illustrate that U.S. and Chinese firms largely do not compete in similar sectors in Ghana.[4] According to available data on World Bank contracts from 2001 through 2011, U.S. and Chinese firms won nearly the same number of contracts, but Chinese firms won significantly more contract dollars (see fig. 16). Chinese and U.S. firms did not appear to overlap in competing for consulting and construction services contracts but overlapped in providing three types of goods: educational, electrical, and transportation equipment. Although contracts for electrical equipment made up nearly 14 percent of the value of contracts for Chinese firms, the same category constituted less than 2 percent of the value of U.S. firms' contracts. Contracts for educational or transportation equipment did not represent a significant portion of the value of contracts for which both U.S. and

---

[4]Services provided by U.S. firms under World Bank–funded contracts represent a small fraction (less than 1 percent) of annual U.S. trade in service exports to Ghana. However, World Bank contracts represent one of the few instances where data are available for examination of potential competition between U.S. and Chinese firms. According to the World Bank, the data include only contracts reviewed by World Bank staff prior to award, which constitute about 40 percent of total World Bank investment lending. The nationality of a firm reflects the country where it is registered, although the firm's parent may be headquartered in another country.

Chinese firms competed. Chinese firms primarily provided electrical equipment and construction services and materials, while U.S. firms primarily provided information technology equipment, management and technical advice, and policy and strategy consulting services.

Figure 16: World Bank–Financed Contracts Won by Firms from the United States, China, and Other Countries in Ghana, 2001-2011

Firm's country of origin	Number of contracts	World Bank contract dollars won, percentage	Contract value by categories, dollars in millions	Top three contract types, number of contracts
United States	39	1	$5 $5	Equipment, information technology .... 7 Management and technical advice .... 5 Feasibility studies[a] 4
China	38	15	$121 $36	Equipment, electricial .... 13 Construction services, installation .... 8 Construction services, maintenance and rehabilitation 6
Other countries[b]	1161	84	$137 $426 $296	Construction services, infrastructure .... 178 Equipment, transportation .... 103 Management and technical advice 97

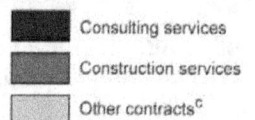

Consulting services

Construction services

Other contracts[c]

Source: GAO analysis of World Bank data.

Notes: According to the World Bank, the data shown include only contracts reviewed by World Bank staff prior to award. In general, these types of contracts constitute about 40 percent of total World Bank investment lending. The nationality of a firm reflects the country in which it is registered, although the firm's parent may be headquartered in another country.

[a]In addition to winning contracts for feasibility studies, U.S. firms won four contracts for educational equipment and four contracts for policy and strategy services.

[b]Other contracts primarily include goods such as transportation equipment, information technology equipment, and electrical equipment.

[c]Firms from at least 32 other countries won World Bank contracts, with firms from Ghana and the United Kingdom winning the most contracts.

Commerce data for U.S. firms competing for host-government contracts in Ghana provide some evidence that U.S. firms competed with Chinese firms almost as often as with firms of other nationalities (see fig. 17). From August 2002 until February 2012, U.S. firms requested assistance from Commerce's Advocacy Center in competing for 11 Ghanaian government contracts for goods and services. U.S. firms competed against Chinese, French, and Israeli firms, respectively, in 4 of the 11 contracts and against German and Ghanaian firms, respectively, for 5 contracts. U.S. and Chinese firms competed for contracts in the telecommunications, computers and information technology, and transportation sectors. U.S. firms competed against firms of other nationalities in sectors that included telecommunications and aerospace.

Figure 17: Nationality of Firms Competing for 11 Ghanaian Government Contracts for Goods and Services, 2002-2012

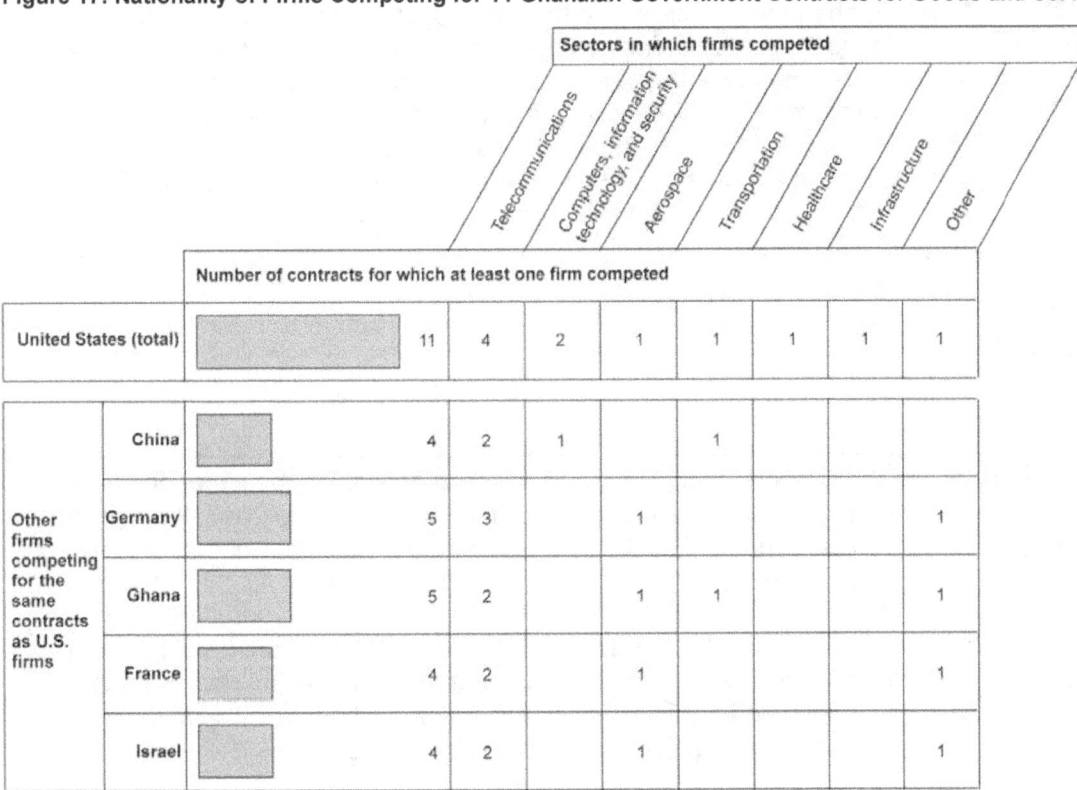

		Number of contracts for which at least one firm competed	Telecommunications	Computers, information technology, and security	Aerospace	Transportation	Healthcare	Infrastructure	Other
United States (total)			11	4	2	1	1	1	1	1
Other firms competing for the same contracts as U.S. firms	China		4	2	1		1			
	Germany		5	3		1				1
	Ghana		5	2		1	1			1
	France		4	2		1				1
	Israel		4	2		1				1

Source: GAO analysis of Department of Commerce data.

Notes: Data shown are for eleven Ghanaian government contracts for which U.S. firms requested Commerce advocacy assistance in August 2002 through February 2012. "Other firms" consists of firms that competed for the largest numbers of contracts. In addition to Chinese firms, firms from Germany, Ghana, France, and Israel competed with U.S. firms for the largest numbers of contracts.

Chinese firms have reportedly followed Ghanaian hiring requirements and implemented quality construction projects in a timely manner. According to U.S. and Ghanaian officials, Ghana's local content requirements regarding hiring of local labor limit the hiring of foreign workers, with exceptions made for some high-skilled areas such as engineering. Data available from Ghana's Ministry of Roads and Highways on certain projects implemented by Chinese firms provide evidence that Ghanaian workers constitute the majority of workers hired by Chinese contractors for construction projects. Additionally, according to MCC data, Chinese contractors working on MCC-funded projects in Ghana hired seven local workers for every Chinese worker. Ghanaian officials who provided oversight of MCC-funded and other projects in Ghana did not report any concerns with Chinese contractors in regard to hiring local labor. Furthermore, officials said that large-scale construction projects implemented by Chinese firms were timely and met quality standards, and Chinese contractors were more accommodating of contract changes compared to other contractors. MCC officials said that the use of an engineering firm to supervise construction projects implemented by a Chinese firm was important to ensuring the quality of work completed.

U.S. and Chinese Grants and Loans to Ghana

U.S. Government's Grants to Ghana Exceeded China's in Recent Years

The U.S. government's grant commitments to Ghana exceeded China's during the period 2006 through 2010. From 2001 to 2010, the United States committed about $1.6 billion in aid in the form of grants to Ghana, including nearly $1.3 billion beginning in 2006 (see fig. 18). The level and composition of U.S. aid has varied, with a sharp 1-year increase in 2007 primarily due to funding from MCC for its $547 million, 5-year compact that focused on agriculture, transportation, and rural services projects.[5] U.S. funding for health assistance generally increased from 2006 to 2010, primarily in the area of antimalaria assistance.

---

[5]MCC compact funds are committed up front when compacts are signed with the partner country and obligated after a compact enters into force.

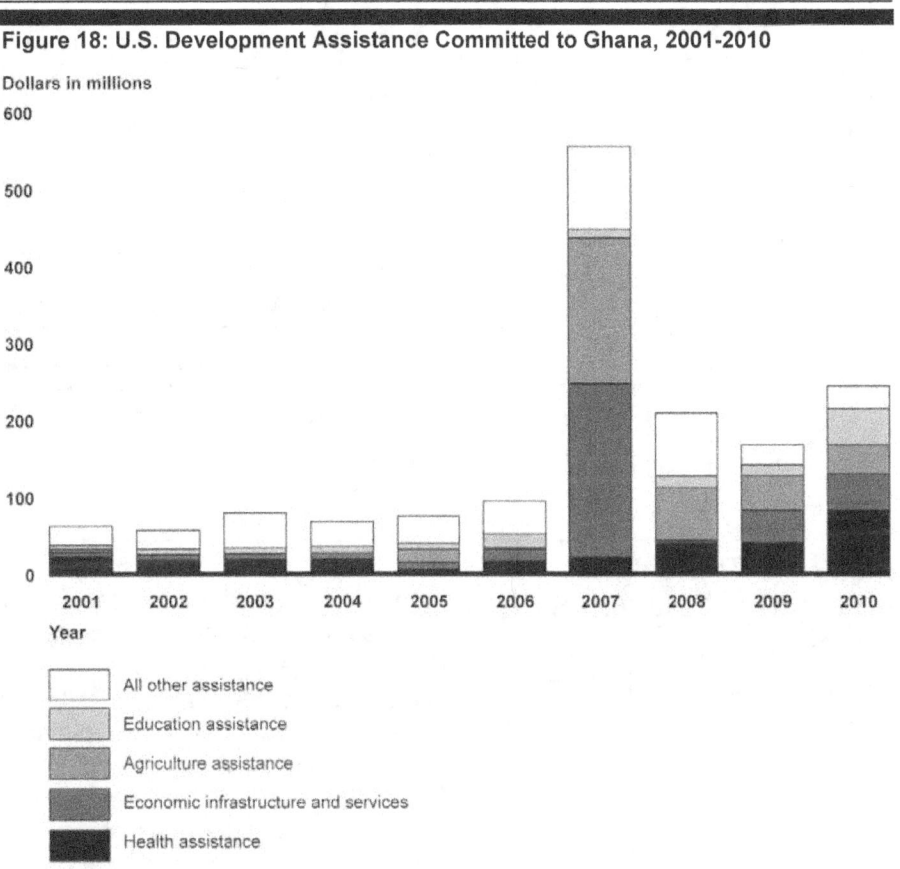

Figure 18: U.S. Development Assistance Committed to Ghana, 2001-2010

Source: GAO analysis of data from USAID.

Note: Commitments are shown in nominal dollars by calendar year.

China has not published information on its grant-based aid to Ghana.
However, data published by the Ghanaian government indicate that
China committed approximately $18 million in grants in 2007, 2008, and
2011, mostly for the construction of Ghana's Ministry of Foreign Affairs
complex (see table 3).

Table 3: China's Grant Commitments to Ghana, 2006-2011

Dollars in millions

Types of projects	Year committed	Grants committed
Economic and technical cooperation	2007	$2.10
	2008	1.26
Subtotal		**$3.36**
Construction of Ministry of Foreign Affairs complex	2011	15.00
Total		**$18.36**

Source: GAO analysis of data from Ghana's Ministry of Finance and Economic Planning.

Notes: The Ghanaian government published data on China's grant commitments in annual budget documents from 2006 through 2011. According to these documents, the published data are for commitments through the end of September for each year.

U.S. Government Committed Smaller Amounts of Loans for Ghana Than China Did in Recent Years

From 2001 to 2011, the U.S. government committed approximately $1.1 billion in loans and related financing to support exports of U.S. goods and services and U.S. firms' investments in Ghana, as shown in figure 19. During this period, U.S. Ex-Im committed about $719 million (64 percent) in loans and other financing for U.S.-made products, including motor vehicles and cars, metal ore mining, and other machinery and equipment. OPIC committed about $399 million (36 percent) in loans and other financing for U.S. firms' investments in areas such as medical equipment, home loans, and the petroleum and minerals sectors.

Figure 19: U.S. Government Loans and Related Financing Committed for U.S-Made Products and U.S. Firms' Investments in Ghana, 2001-2011

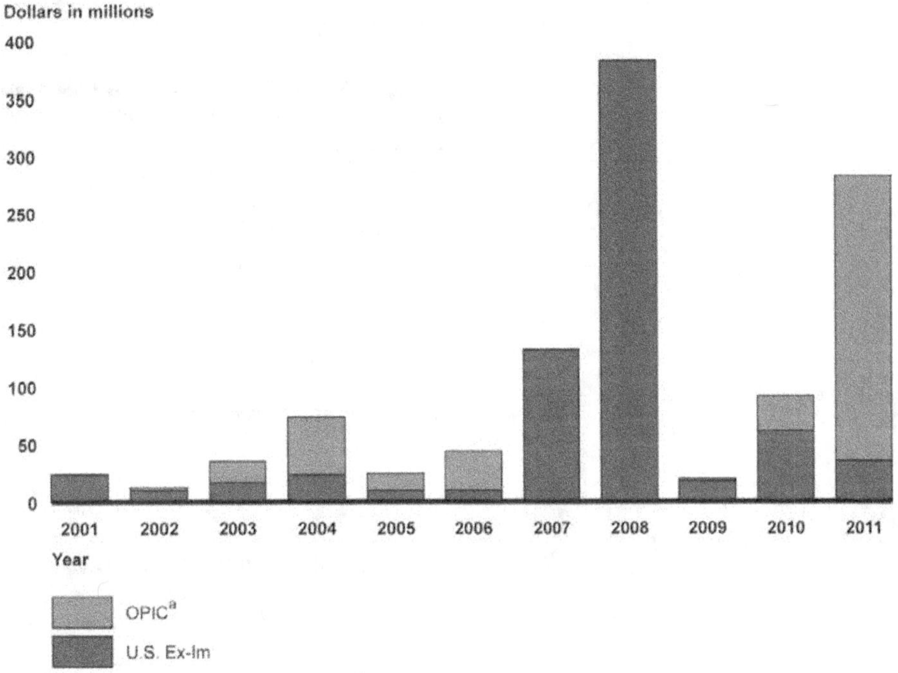

Dollars in millions

Source: GAO analysis of data from U.S. Ex-Im and OPIC.

Notes: Data shown are for nominal dollars by calendar year. In addition, these values are shown by calendar year, although U.S. Ex-Im and OPIC typically report data by fiscal year.

[a]OPIC may report data for some financing commitments, such as investment funds, only at the regional level. Data shown do not reflect OPIC investment funds for regional use in sub-Saharan Africa, possibly including Ghana. According to OPIC officials, because recipients of OPIC investment assistance may choose to invest in a set of countries, OPIC may initially lack information such as the countries where investments are made. In addition, according to OPIC officials, in countries with limited investment activity, business confidentiality agreements may prevent the disclosure of data that would reveal details of individual transactions.

Comprehensive information on China's loans to Ghana is not available, but according to data published by the government of Ghana, China committed, or agreed to, more than $3 billion in loans to Ghana between 2006 and 2011. As shown in table 4, China's loans were primarily for infrastructure construction, including a dam and other energy infrastructure; the installation of an electrification system; and communications technology. China committed its largest loan to Ghana in 2011, when the China Development Bank signed an agreement with the Ghanaian government to provide $3 billion, largely for oil and gas infrastructure and transportation infrastructure, including a railway, ports, and harbors. Chinese firms and materials are to make up about 60 percent of the content used under this agreement, which will be bid competitively among Chinese firms, according to a Ghanaian official. Repayment of some Chinese loans is tied to natural resources, such as oil and cocoa.[6]

Table 4: China's Loans Committed to Ghana, 2006-2011

Dollars in millions

Types of projects	Year committed	Loans committed
Bui hydro electric project	2008	$68.04
	2009	61.83
	2010	54.96
Subtotal		**$184.83**
Communication system for national security	2008	6.29
	2009	5.71
	2010	.74
Subtotal		**$12.74**
Economic and technical cooperation	2007	10.00
	2008	6.00
	2009	5.45
	2010	.96
Subtotal		**$22.41**
E-government project	2010	33.00
Information and communication technology	2010	2.58
National communication infrastructure	2007	3.80
	2008	4.58
	2010	.62
Subtotal		**$9.00**
Supply of Installation of Self-Help Electrification Program	2008	12.30
	2009	11.18
	2010	2.07

[6]According to information published by the government of Ghana, the terms of China's $3 billion loan to Ghana indicate that a Chinese state-owned oil company will purchase crude oil from Ghana's national petroleum company to support repayment of the loan. A Ghanaian ministry official said that oil also would be used as collateral on the loan. According to a World Bank report, cocoa exports make up part of the repayment of China's loan for the construction of the Bui Dam in Ghana.

Dollars in millions

Types of projects	Year committed	Loans committed
Subtotal		**$25.55**
Support for fisheries sector	2008	18.00
	2009	21.27
	2010	23.40
Subtotal		**$62.67**
Various infrastructure development projects[a]	2011	3,000.00
Total		**$3,352.78**

Source: GAO analysis of data published by Ghana's Ministry of Finance and Economic Planning.

Notes: The Ghanaian government published data on China's loan commitments in annual budget documents from 2006 through 2011. Documents largely state that published data are for commitments through the end of September for that year.

[a]Available budget data did not include China's $3 billion loan to Ghana signed in December 2011; however, we included this loan in our analysis because this financing represents China's most significant loan package to Ghana.

U.S. and Chinese Investments in Ghana

Data on the United States' foreign direct investments in Ghana suggest that U.S. foreign direct investment flows exceeded China's reported foreign direct investment flows in the most recent years for which comparable data are available.[7] In the 2-year period 2010 through 2011, U.S. cumulative foreign direct investment was $808 million; in the 5-year period 2007 through 2011, China's reported cumulative foreign direct investment was $158 million (see fig. 20). According to experts, data on

---

[7]BEA has not released U.S. foreign direct investment flows to Ghana from 2007 to 2009 for reasons of confidentiality.

China's foreign direct investment are likely underreported,[8] and according to BEA, data on U.S. foreign direct investment may also be underreported,[9] limiting precise comparisons of the United States' and China's investments. According to information from BEA, from 2006 through 2011, the vast majority of U.S. foreign direct investment stock was in mining and activities related to the mining sector, with an average annual growth rate of 25 percent in mining investments during that period. This growth was a turnaround from the decline in U.S. foreign direct investment stock in mining from 2001 through 2005. Comparable information on China's foreign direct investment in Ghana by sector is not available.

---

[8]According to experts, Chinese firms set up subsidiaries, in places such as Hong Kong and the British Virgin Islands, that can be used to make investments in sub-Saharan Africa. Such investments are not captured by China's data on foreign direct investment and may be a significant source of underreporting. In addition, many small and medium-sized enterprises may not register their foreign direct investments, which therefore may not be reflected in China's data. According to an International Monetary Fund (IMF) working paper, China's foreign direct investment data also show inconsistencies between investment flows and changes in investment stock that are difficult to explain (see Montfort Mlachila and Misa Takebe, "FDI from BRICs to LICs: Emerging Growth Driver?" *IMF Working Paper*, WP/11/178 [2011], 11). Finally, China does not define foreign direct investment when reporting its data. However, the types of data China reports for its foreign direct investments (e.g., equity investment data, reinvested earnings data) are similar to data reported for U.S. foreign direct investment. However, China's reported foreign direct investment data represent official information published by the Chinese government and, despite their limitations, have been used in various reports, including those published by international organizations (e.g., the IMF), government agencies, academic experts, and other research institutions, to describe China's foreign direct investment activities in Africa.

[9]BEA noted that these data may not include investments in Sub-Saharan Africa by U.S. firms through subsidiaries in locations such as the Netherlands. According to BEA, U.S. foreign direct investment data are based on a 2009 benchmark survey that covers the value of all U.S. foreign direct investment, but these data may not reflect foreign direct investments by smaller firms.

Figure 20: Reported Flows of Foreign Direct Investment from the United States and China to Ghana, 2007-2011

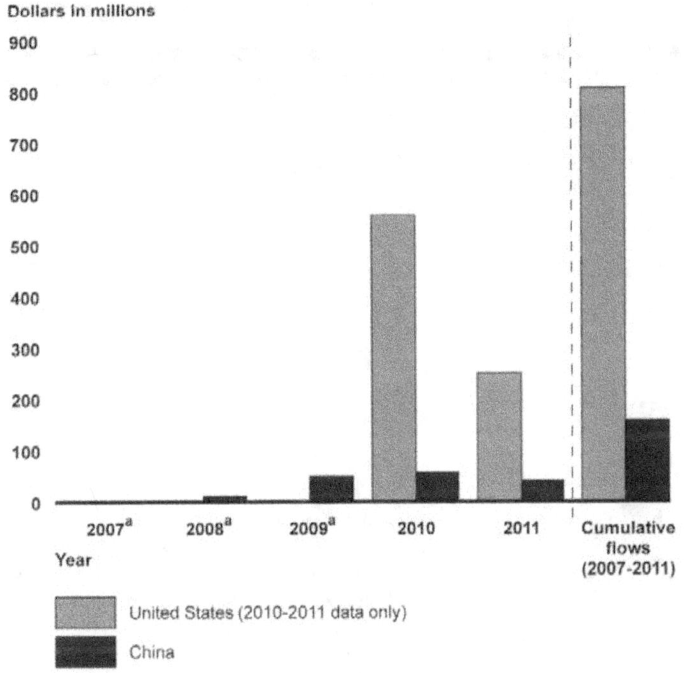

Dollars in millions

United States (2010-2011 data only)

China

Source: GAO analysis of data from BEA, China's Ministry of Commerce, China's National Bureau of Statistics, and Haver Analytics.

Notes: Data are shown in nominal values.

[a]Data on U.S. foreign direct investment flows from 2007 through 2009 are confidential and have not been released.

Data on the purchase of ownership interests in oil blocks in Ghana as of August 2012 indicate that U.S. firms are active in the petroleum sector but that Chinese firms are not (see fig. 21). Following a U.S. firm's discovery of oil offshore in Ghana in 2007, commercial production began in late 2010, and Ghana became an oil-exporting country in 2011. U.S. companies have operator roles in 2 of Ghana's 17 oil blocks, with primary responsibility for operations such as drilling, maintenance, and complying with required rules and regulations. In addition, U.S. firms have purchased ownership interests in 4 oil blocks as nonoperators, where these firms have a minority stake and are not responsible for operations.[10] Chinese firms do not operate or own any shares of Ghana's oil blocks. European and African firms operate the majority of the remaining oil blocks.

Figure 21: Numbers and Types of U.S. and Chinese Firms' Investments in Oil Blocks in Ghana, August 2012

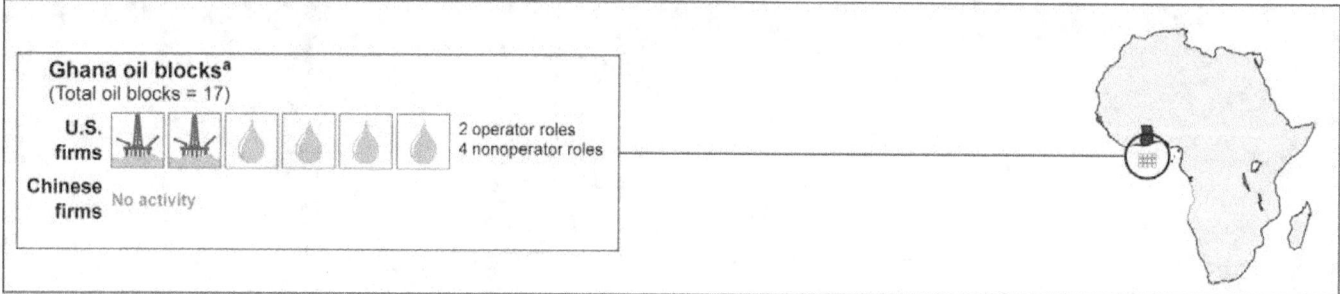

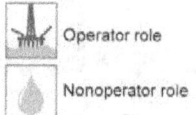 Operator role

Nonoperator role

Source: GAO analysis of data from the U.S. Department of Energy and the government of Ghana (data); MapInfo (map).

[a]In addition to U.S. firms, firms from Bermuda, Italy, Nigeria, and the United Kingdom, among others, operate Ghana's 17 oil blocks. In one oil block, a U.S. firm had an operator role and another U.S. firm had a nonoperator role.

---

[10]In one oil block in Ghana, one U.S. firm was in an operator role and another U.S. firm was in a nonoperator role.

Case Study of U.S. and Chinese Engagement in Kenya

U.S. and Chinese Trade with Kenya

China's Trade in Goods with Kenya Has Increased

China's total trade in goods with Kenya has increased since 2001 and has exceeded U.S. total trade since 2007 (see fig. 22). From 2001 to 2011, total U.S. trade in goods fluctuated but changed relatively little overall, rising from nearly $711 million in 2001 to $844 million in 2011; although U.S. imports nearly tripled, U.S. exports declined by about 20 percent. China's total trade grew by a factor of 17 during this period, from nearly $145 million to approximately $2.4 billion, primarily because of the increase in Chinese exports to Kenya.

Figure 22: U.S. and Chinese Total Trade in Goods with Kenya, 2001-2011

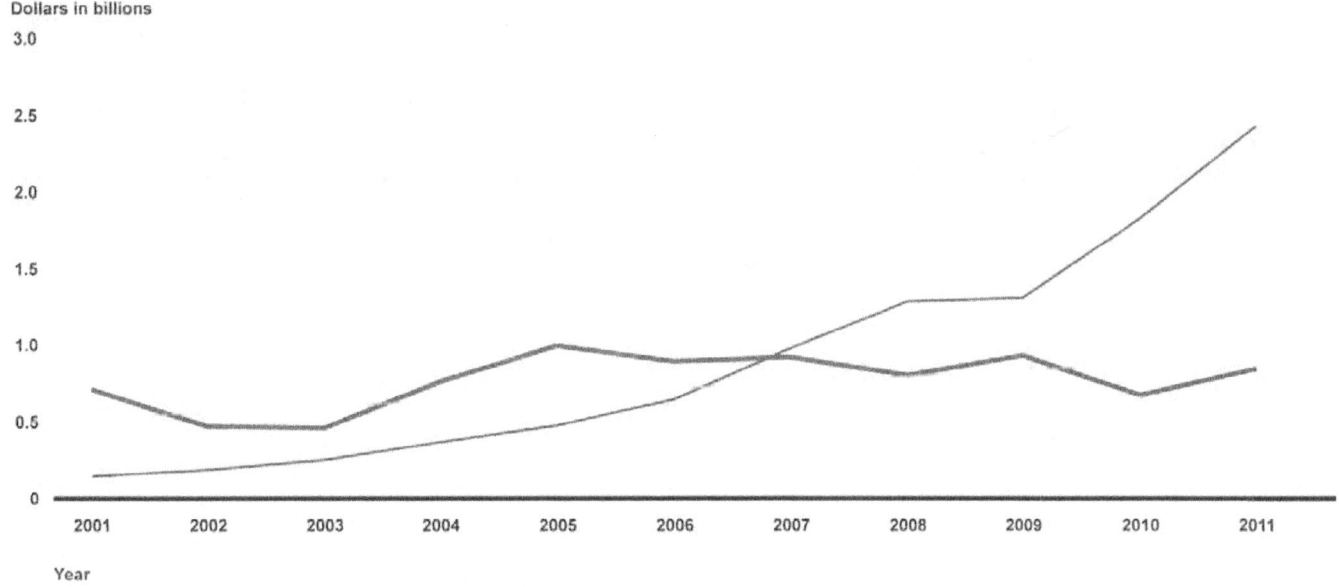

Source: GAO analysis of UN data.

Notes: Total trade is defined as imports plus exports. Trade data are shown in nominal dollars. Changes in value over time are due in part to changes in the prices of traded goods. For consistency with data reported by the IMF's Direction of Trade Statistics and the World Trade Atlas, data for Chinese imports have been adjusted to exclude imports of a category of goods labeled "special transactions."

From 2001 through 2011, U.S. exports to Kenya decreased while Chinese exports rose, as shown in figure 23. Specifically, U.S. exports to

Kenya dropped from $574 million in 2001 to $447 million in 2011, primarily owing to a decline in U.S exports of machinery and transport equipment.[1] Meanwhile, Chinese exports to Kenya in 2011 greatly exceeded the United States', growing from nearly $139 million in 2001 to $2.4 billion in 2011. In 2011, China's top exports included manufactured goods (e.g., woven fabrics and footwear), and machinery and transport equipment (e.g., transmission equipment and motorcycles).

Figure 23: U.S. and Chinese Exports of Goods to Kenya, 2001- 2011

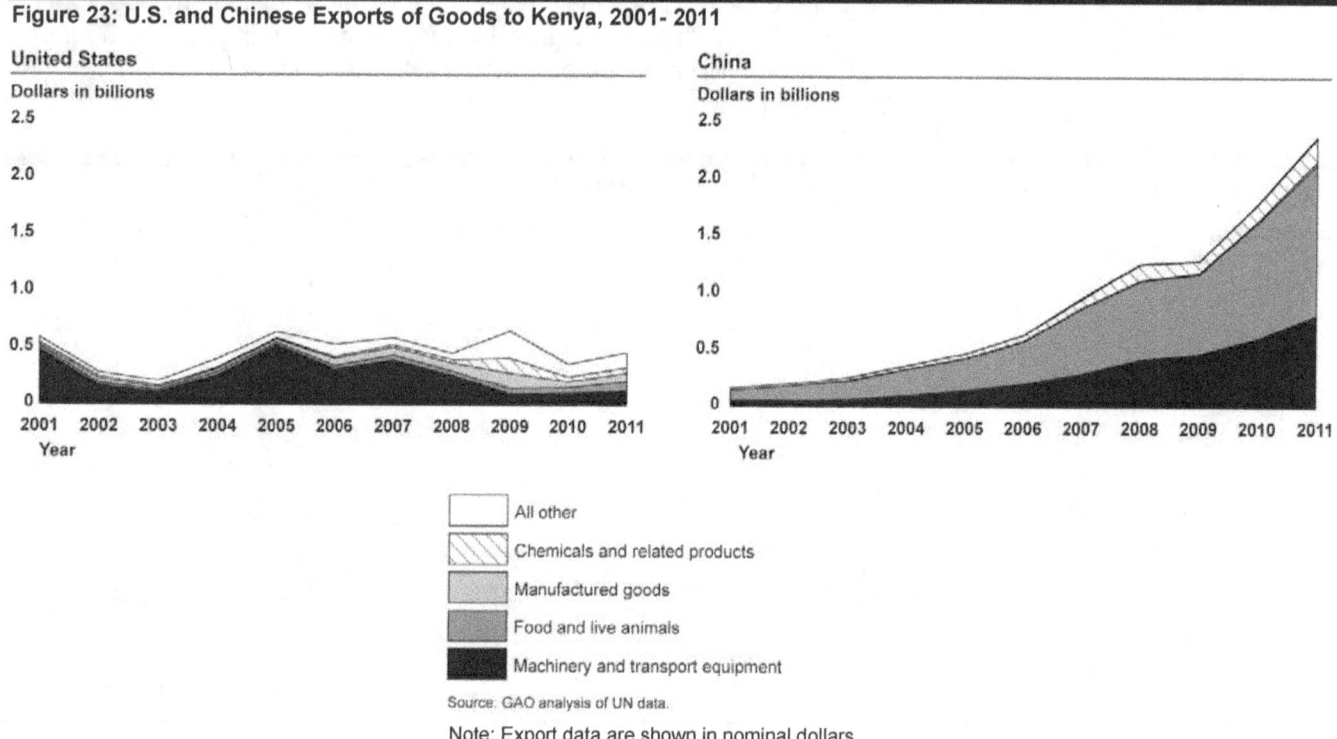

Source: GAO analysis of UN data.

Note: Export data are shown in nominal dollars.

In contrast to exports, U.S. imports of goods from Kenya exceeded Chinese imports in 2001 through 2011. U.S. and Chinese imports of goods differed in size and composition, as shown in figure 24. U.S. imports nearly tripled from 2001 to 2011, from $137 million to $397

---

[1]U.S. exports of machinery and transport equipment declined from $469 million in 2001 to $110 million in 2011. This category includes exports of aircraft and related equipment, which dropped from $413 million in 2001 to $6 million in 2011.

million, in part because of an increase in imports of apparel and clothing
from $69 million in 2001 to $272 million in 2011.

Figure 24: U.S. and Chinese Imports of Goods from Kenya, 2001-2011

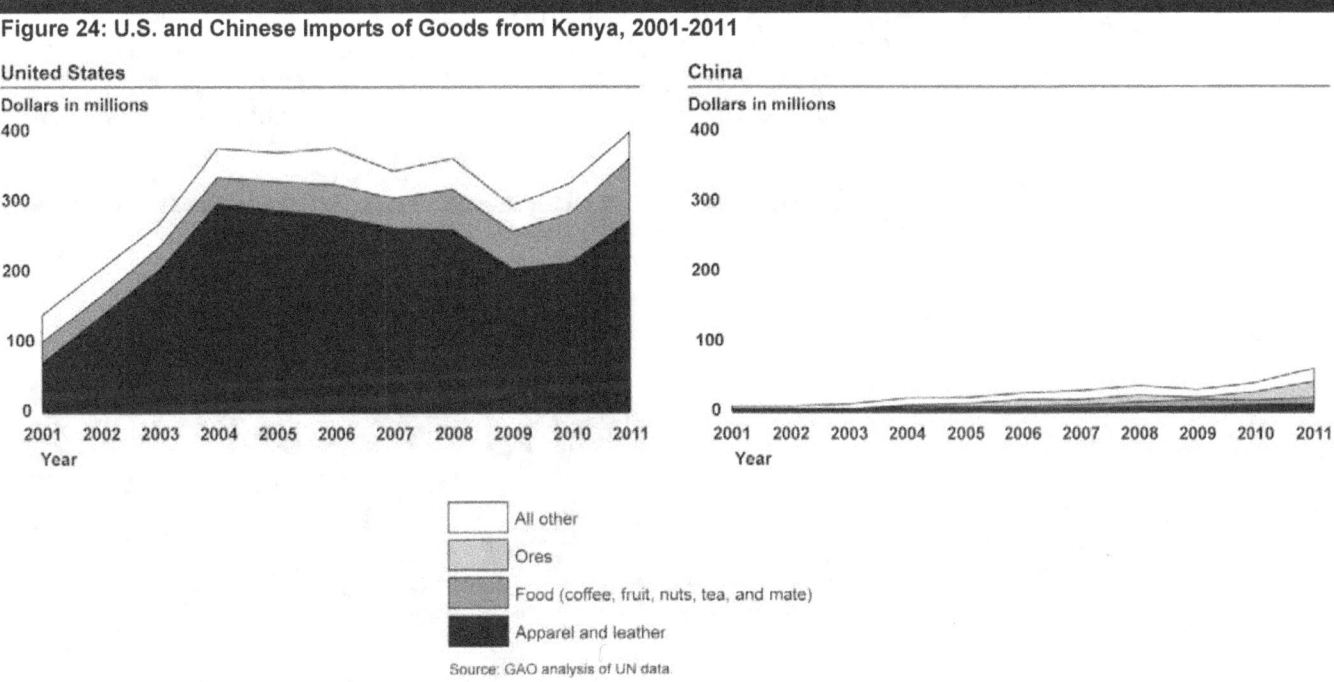

Source: GAO analysis of UN data.

Note: Import data are shown in nominal dollars.

Under AGOA, the U.S. trade preference program, textiles, apparel,
leather, and footwear constituted nearly 96 percent of U.S. imports from
Kenya from 2001 to 2011 (see fig. 25).[2] AGOA's "third-country fabric
provision" has enabled Kenya to generally increase its apparel exports,
according to U.S. and Kenyan officials, and Kenya has become one of the
largest exporters of nonpetroleum goods to the United States. U.S. and
Kenyan officials pointed to the positive employment effects in Kenya
associated with apparel exports under AGOA. However, they also noted
AGOA's limited success in enabling Kenya and other sub-Saharan
African countries to manufacture textiles and fabrics, which form the input
for apparel manufacturing. Kenya and Ghana obtain fabrics mostly from

---

[2]From 2001 to 2011, approximately $2.4 billion in U.S. imports from Kenya—
approximately 75 percent of total U.S. imports from the country in that period— had tariffs
eliminated under AGOA and GSP combined.

China and other Asian countries to manufacture apparel for export to the United States, according to U.S. officials in these countries. As a result, Chinese exports of textile and fabrics to Kenya also increased during this period, from $40 million in 2001 to $347 million in 2011. Meanwhile, Chinese imports from Kenya were less than U.S. imports but grew at a faster rate, from nearly $6 million in 2001 to almost $60 million in 2011. Top Chinese imports in 2011 included iron ore, leather, scrap metal, and tea.

Figure 25: U.S. Imports of Goods from Kenya under AGOA, 2001-2011

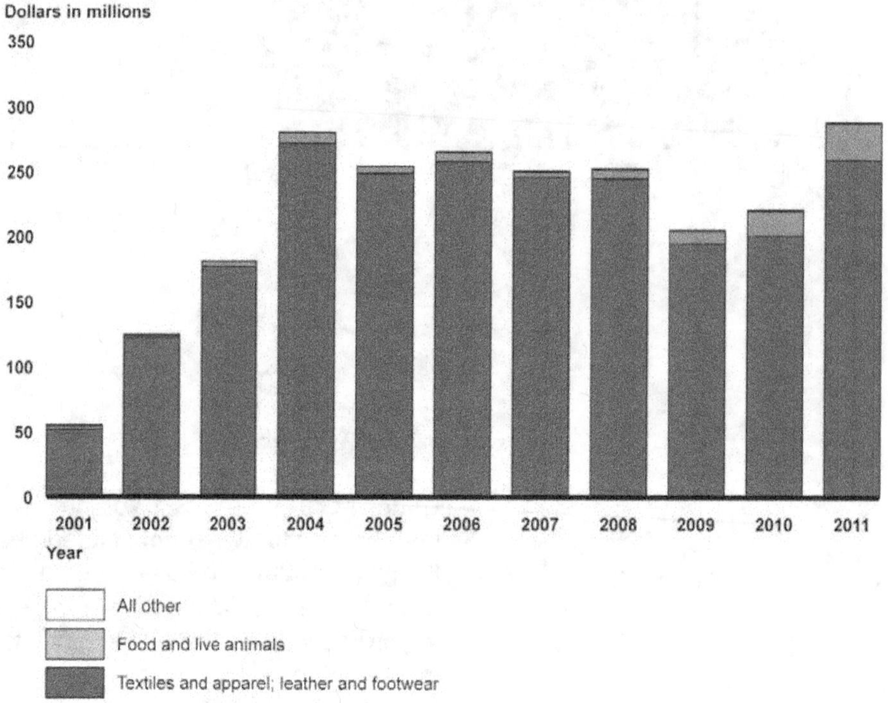

Dollars in millions

Source: GAO analysis of Department of Commerce data.

Notes: Data are shown in nominal dollars. U.S. imports of goods represented as "all other," ranging from a low of approximately $35,000 in 2003 to a high of nearly $1.13 million in 2011, are not visible.

U.S. Trade in Services with Kenya Is Estimated at Nearly $1 Billion Annually, but Comparable Data on China's Trade in Services Are Not Available

From 2006 through 2011, total U.S. trade in services with Kenya averaged about $899 million annually. U.S. imports of services, not including travel and passenger fares, averaged about $281 million per year, and U.S. exports of services averaged about $618 million per year.[3] The largest sector for U.S. imports of services was business, professional, and technical services. The largest sectors for U.S. exports of services were business, professional, and technical services; education; and travel and passenger fares. Comparable country-level data on China's trade in services in Kenya are not available.

U.S. and Chinese Firms Compete in Some Sectors but Generally Not for Donor-Funded and Host-Government Contracts

Competition in Information- and Communication-Technology Sector

Chinese firms are competing with U.S. firms in Kenya's information- and communication-technology sector. Additionally, counterfeits manufactured by Chinese firms adversely affect U.S. firms' sales and reputation in Kenya. However, U.S. and Chinese firms largely do not compete in similar sectors in Kenya for donor-funded and host-government contracts.

Chinese firms are competing with U.S. firms in Kenya's information- and communication-technology sector, but it is not clear whether this competition directly affects U.S.-made exports to these countries, according to officials of U.S. agencies and U.S. firms operating in Kenya. A senior official at a large U.S. information- and communication-technology firm noted that Chinese firms are innovating and adapting quickly to local markets. For example, a Chinese firm in this sector has established one of the largest training centers in Kenya. Moreover, this official noted that in contrast to the U.S. government, the Chinese government and European governments are more active in combining

---

[3]Data on U.S imports of travel and passenger fares to Kenya are unavailable and are not included in the estimates for total U.S. trade in services and imports of services. However, given that Kenya received more U.S. travelers than Ghana in 2010, according to the Kenyan Ministry of Tourism and U.S. Department of Homeland Security, we estimate that U.S. imports from Kenya of travel and passenger fares in 2006 through 2010 likely equaled or exceeded this category of U.S. imports from Ghana, which averaged $350 million per year during that period. From 2006 to 2011, annual U.S. imports averaged approximately $50 million to $200 million per year from Kenya for business, professional, and technical services. During the same period, annual U.S. exports to Kenya averaged around $50 million to $200 million for business, professional, and technical services, $176 million for education services, and $109 million for travel and passenger fares. To calculate total trade, imports, and exports to Kenya, we used the higher value when ranges of estimates were provided for service sectors such as business, professional, and technical services. Our estimates are based on underlying tabulations from BEA and other sources and on our analysis of BEA's survey data.

government and business interests to take advantage of large telecommunications projects in countries such as Kenya. Trade data indicate that China's exports of telecommunications equipment to Kenya rose from $0.5 million in 2001 to $122 million in 2011. However, it is unclear whether direct competition from Chinese firms affects U.S.-made exports, in part because multinational corporations headquartered in the United States operate globally. For example, according to a representative of a U.S. firm that manufactures telecommunications equipment, most of its products are manufactured outside the United States and therefore competition from Chinese telecommunications firms in Kenya does not affect U.S.-made exports.

Impact of Counterfeits from China

Counterfeit goods and related products from China have adversely affected U.S. firms' sales and reputation in Kenya.[4] According to a 2012 study by the Kenyan Association of Manufacturers, counterfeit goods primarily from China, especially in the energy, electronic, and electrical components sector, have negatively affected the sales and reputation of U.S. firms and others with operations in Kenya.[5] For example, according to a representative of a U.S. firm that manufactures dry-cell batteries in Kenya, the influx of counterfeit and substandard products, mainly from China, caused the U.S. firm's business to decline, and over time the firm has decreased the number of its employees in Kenya from 800 to 300. Furthermore, according to the former head of the U.S. firm's East Africa division, prior to competition from Chinese products, the U.S. firm's market share of carbon zinc batteries was about 80 percent. However, by May 2011, Chinese products controlled 60 percent of the market. This official also noted that in some cases, Chinese products, although of poorer quality, mimicked the U.S. firm's product branding and color schemes. Although the U.S. firm successfully litigated in Kenyan courts against this trademark infraction, according to this official the penalty was

---

[4]According to a March 2012 draft report by the Kenyan Association of Manufacturers, counterfeiting includes the violation of trademarks, industrial designs, geographical indications, copyright, and related rights. Kenyan Association of Manufacturers, *The Study to Determine Severity of the Counterfeit Problem In Kenya as It Affects Industries and Impact of Proliferation of Counterfeit Products from Other EAC Partner States And Far East Countries Into the Kenyan Market*, draft report (March 2012).

[5]The Kenyan Association of Manufacturers report also notes that manufacturers in Kenya lose more than $40 million annually because of counterfeit products. According to manufacturers interviewed for the report, about 30 percent of electrical components and electronics (such as motors and generators, switchgears, and batteries) sold in Kenya are counterfeits and are primarily from China.

too lenient to have a deterrent effect on the Chinese manufacturers of counterfeits. Trade data indicate that China's exports of batteries (including rechargeable batteries and parts) increased from $15 million in 2001 to $48 million in 2011. To combat Chinese counterfeits, the U.S. embassy in Kenya has sponsored several public-education programs, and the U.S. government is providing technical assistance to Kenya's Anti-Counterfeit Agency, established in 2010. However, corruption in Kenya, as well as the Kenyan government's lack of willingness to take appropriate actions, have significantly impeded the fight against counterfeits, according to U.S. firms and the Kenyan private sector.[6]

General Absence of Competition for Donor-Funded and Host-Government Contracts

U.S. and Chinese firms largely do not compete with each other in similar sectors in Kenya for donor-funded and Kenyan government contracts, including contracts for the provision of goods and services. According to data on World Bank-funded projects in Kenya for which U.S. and Chinese firms won contracts between 2001 and 2011, Chinese firms won a larger share of contract dollars and were primarily active in providing medical equipment and construction services and materials.[7] In contrast, U.S. firms won a significantly smaller share of overall contract dollars for World Bank–funded projects in Kenya and were primarily active in consulting services, such as providing management and technical advice and supervising construction. Figure 26 compares World Bank-funded contracts won by firms from the United States, China, and other countries.

---

[6]Although Kenya established an anticounterfeit agency in 2010, a representative for U.S. firms in Kenya and Kenyan officials noted that the agency has been underresourced and is unable to take necessary actions against counterfeits.

[7]Services provided by U.S. firms under World Bank–funded contracts represent a small fraction (less than 1 percent) of annual U.S. trade in service exports to Kenya. However, World Bank contracts represent one of the few instances where data are available for examination of potential competition between U.S. and Chinese firms. According to the World Bank, the data include only contracts reviewed by World Bank staff prior to award, which constitute about 40 percent of total World Bank investment lending. The nationality of a firm reflects the country where it is registered, although the firm's parent may be headquartered in another country.

Figure 26: World Bank–Funded Contracts Won by Firms from the United States, China, and Other Countries in Kenya, 2001-2011

Firm's country of origin	Number of contracts	World Bank contract dollars won, percentage	Contract value by categories, dollars in millions	Top three contract types, number of contracts
United States	14	⌐ 1	⌐ $8 $1	Management and technical advice .... 7 Construction supervision .... 2 Equipment, information technology 1
China	25	28	⌐ $1 ⌐ $20 $296	Equipment, medical .... 9 Works, maintenance and rehabilitation .... 5 Works, building 2
Other countries[a]	440	71	$126 $537 $145	Management and technical advice .... 58 Feasibility studies .... 35 Equipment, transportation 33

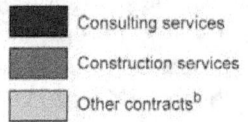

■ Consulting services

▨ Construction services

☐ Other contracts[b]

Source: GAO analysis of World Bank data.

Notes: According to the World Bank, the data shown include only contracts reviewed by World Bank staff prior to award. In general, these types of contracts constitute about 40 percent of total World Bank investment lending. In addition, the nationality of a firm reflects the country in which it is registered, although the firm's parent may be headquartered in another country.

[a]Other contracts primarily include goods such as medical equipment and products, transportation equipment, and water supply and sewerage equipment.

[b]Firms from at least 27 other countries won World Bank contracts, with firms from Kenya and the United Kingdom winning the most contracts.

Officials from the Kenyan government and NGOs generally viewed Chinese firms' implementation of construction projects positively, because their projects were completed in a timely manner and were of better quality than those implemented by local Kenyan companies. According to Kenyan Ministry of Roads officials, Chinese contractors generally met standards for road construction, in part because the contracts included adequate supervision by third parties. Moreover, strong application of local-content rules in Kenya has restricted the number of Chinese workers and led to Chinese contractors' hiring more local workers, according to U.S. and Kenyan government officials. In addition, according to U.S. officials and other donors, Chinese firms' business practices, such as housing workers near project sites and maintaining long work days, contribute to keeping construction costs low. Finally, the presence of Chinese firms, even on projects funded by other donors, has helped create a positive image for China in Kenya, according to U.S. and Kenyan officials. By contrast, the United States may get less publicity despite its large aid commitment, because it does not fund infrastructure projects in

Kenya, according to a U.S. official. Figure 27 shows a newly built highway and signage for the Chinese state-owned firm that constructed the road in Nairobi, Kenya.

Figure 27: Photos of Newly Built Road and Signage for Chinese Contractor That Built Road Section in Nairobi, Kenya

Source: GAO.

Left to right: Chinese firms won contracts for the newly built Nairobi-Thika Highway, funded by the African Development Bank and the Chinese government. Signage of Sinohydro Corporation Limited, one of the three contractors that build the Nairobi-Thika Highway.

Commerce data on U.S. firms bidding on host-government contracts provide some evidence that European firms were U.S. firms' primary competitors for host-government contracts. From August 2002 to February 2012, U.S. firms requested assistance from Commerce's Advocacy Center in competing for 28 Kenyan government contracts for goods and services. Chinese firms competed on 4 of these contracts, for oil and gas, medical equipment, healthcare, and computers and information technology equipment (see fig. 28). French, British, and Dutch firms competed with U.S. firms for more contracts and in more sectors, including aerospace, oil and gas, energy and power, and services, than did Chinese firms.

Figure 28: Nationality of Firms Competing for 28 Kenyan Government Contracts for Goods and Services, 2002–2012

Sectors in which firms competed

Number of contracts for which at least one firm competed

	Number of contracts	Computers, information technology, and security	Aerospace	Energy and power	Services	Oil and gas	Other	Healthcare	Telecommunications	Infrastructure	Transportation
United States (total)	28	5	4	4	4	3	3	2	1	1	1
China	4	1				1	1	1			
France	8	1	2		2	2			1		
United Kingdom	7	3	1	1		1	1				
Netherlands	6	1			1	3				1	
South Africa	5	2	1		1	1					
Germany	5	1					1		1	1	1

Other firms competing for the same contracts as U.S. firms

Source: GAO analysis of Department of Commerce data.

Note: Data shown are for 28 Kenyan government contracts for which U.S. firms requested Commerce advocacy assistance in August 2002 through February 2012. Firms from France, the United Kingdom, the Netherlands, South Africa, and Germany competed with U.S. firms for the largest numbers of contracts.

United States' and China's Grants and Loans to Kenya

U.S. Grants to Kenya Exceed China's in Recent Years

The U.S. government committed more grant assistance to Kenya than China did in 2009 and 2010. From 2001 to 2010, the United States committed almost $4 billion in aid to Kenya, including about $1.7 billion beginning in 2009, predominantly in the form of grants (see fig. 29).[8] The level of U.S. aid to Kenya generally increased from 2001 through 2010, largely because of an increase in funding in the health sector through initiatives such as the President's Emergency Plan for AIDS Relief and the President's Malaria Initiative as well as an increase in humanitarian assistance, primarily food aid. U.S. health programs in Kenya are among the largest U.S. government health portfolios globally, according to the Department of State.

[8]According to U.S. aid data reported to OECD, concessional loans comprised about 0.1 percent of U.S. aid to Kenya from 2001 through 2010. The United States has not committed any loans as aid to Kenya since 2008.

Figure 29: U.S. Development Assistance Committed to Kenya, 2001-2010

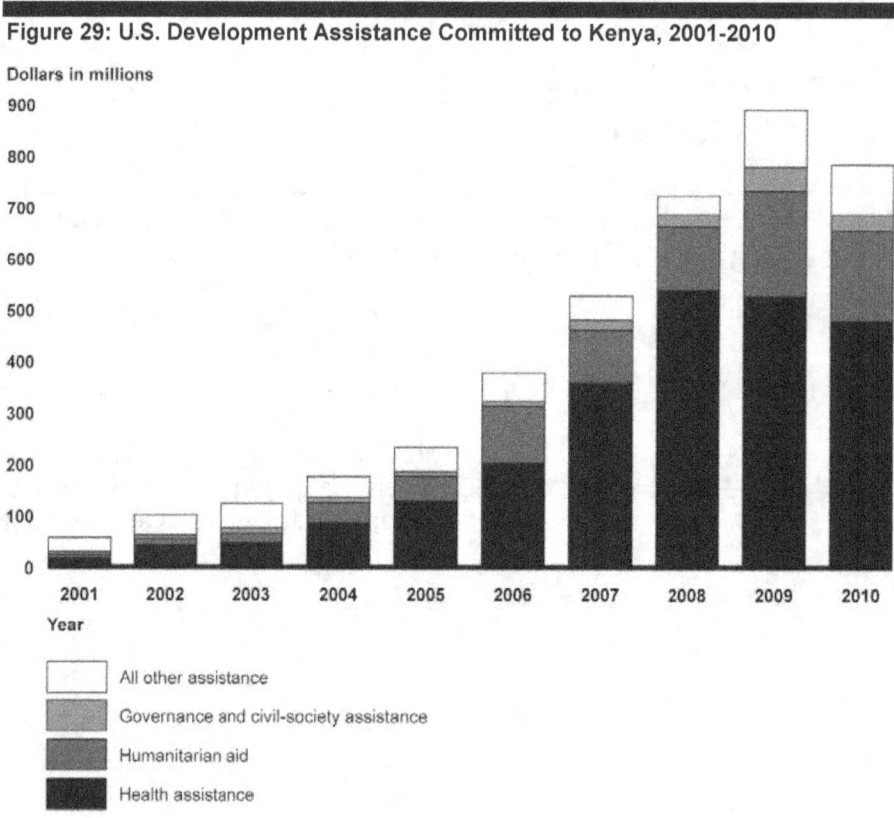

Dollars in millions

Source: GAO analysis of data from USAID.

Note: Import data are reported in nominal dollars.

China does not publish data on its grants to countries, but Kenyan government documents indicate that China committed almost $39 million in grants from July 2009 through June 2012, (see table 5).[9] Most of China's grants were for infrastructure such as roads, a hospital, and a sports center. China also committed assistance for emergency food aid in Kenya's fiscal year 2009/2010.

[9]The Kenyan government reported China's grant commitments for the Kenyan fiscal year (July-June).

Table 5: China's Grants Committed to Kenya, July 2009–June 2012

Types of projects	Year committed[a]	Grants committed
Renovation of Kasarani sports center	2009/2010	$2,927,970
	2010/2011	12,016,970
Subtotal		**$14,944,940**
Construction of hospital in Eastlands	2009/2010	7,092,419
	2010/2011	1,037,388
Subtotal		**$8,129,807**
Gambogi-Serem road	2009/2010	651,877
	2010/2011	606,305
	2011/2012	4,505,242
Subtotal		**$5,763,424**
Rehabilitation of Nairobi roads and street lighting project	2009/2010	3,259,384
Social economic recovery and reconstruction	2009/2010	2,933,445
Emergency food aid	2009/2010	3,146,609
Maize flour processing project	2009/2010	749,111
Total		**$38,926,720**

Source: GAO analysis of Government of Kenya data.

[a]Grant commitments are shown for Kenyan fiscal years (July-June).

U.S. Government Committed Loans for U.S. Exports and Investments in Various Sectors, while China Committed Loans Mainly for Infrastructure Construction

The U.S. government committed about $896 million in loans and related financing, such as loan guarantees and insurance, between 2001 and 2011, primarily to support the export of U.S.-made aerospace products and parts and for U.S. investments in geothermal power and other sectors in Kenya (see fig. 30).[10]

---

[10]From 2001 to 2011, OPIC authorized about $363 million, more than half of which was authorized in 2011 for investment in a geothermal power plant. During this period, U.S. Ex-Im authorized about $533 million, with about 90 percent of those funds authorized for aerospace products and parts.

**Figure 30: U.S. Government Loans and Related Financing Committed for U.S.-made
Products and U.S. Firms' Investments in Kenya, 2001-2011**

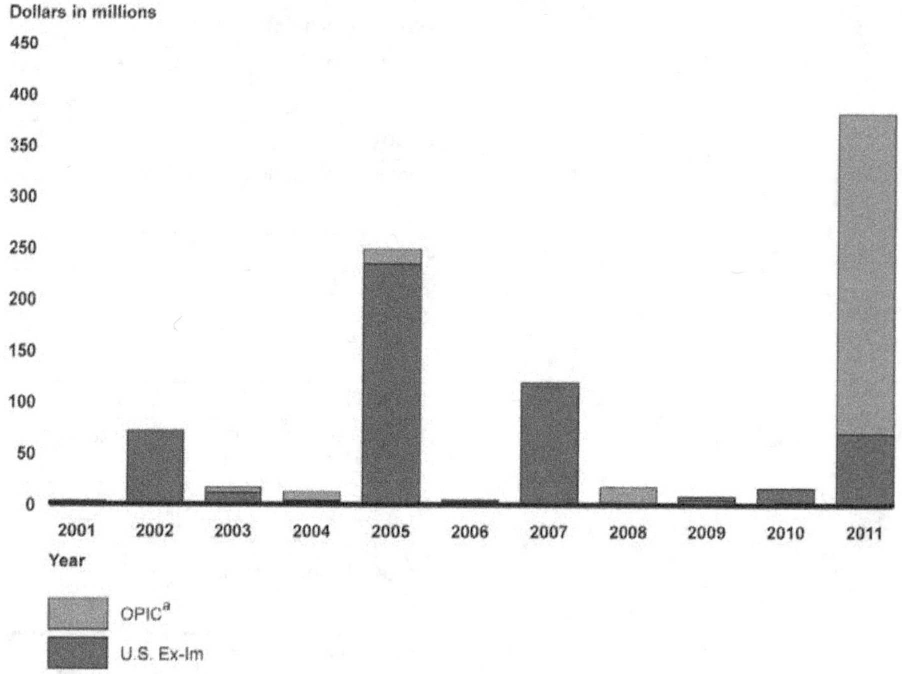

Dollars in millions

Source: GAO analysis of data from U.S. Ex-Im and OPIC.

Notes: Data are shown in nominal dollars by calendar year. In addition, these values are shown by
calendar year, although U.S. Ex-Im and OPIC typically report data by fiscal year.

[a]OPIC may report data for some financing commitments, such as investment funds, only at the
regional level. Data shown do not reflect OPIC investment funds for regional use in sub-Saharan
Africa, possibly including Kenya. According to OPIC officials, because recipients of OPIC investment
assistance may choose to invest in a set of countries, OPIC may initially lack information such as the
countries where investments are made. In addition, according to OPIC officials, in countries with
limited investment activity, business confidentiality agreements may prevent the disclosure of data
that would reveal details of individual transactions.

China authorized about $480 million in loans from July 2009 to June
2012, primarily for infrastructure such as roads, geothermal wells, and
power distribution (see table 6). China also committed funds for an e-
government initiative, upgrading of equipment at universities and training
institutes, rural telecommunication development, and purchase of other
equipment. As a result of its recent funding, China has become one of the
top donors to Kenya in the last 5 years, primarily providing highly
concessional loans, according to a senior official at Kenya's Ministry of
Finance.

Table 6: China's Loans for Projects in Kenya, July 2009–June 2012

Types of projects	Year committed[a]	Loans committed
Nairobi eastern and northern bypass road project	2009/2010	$26,075,070
	2010/2011	54,567,474
	2011/2012	24,778,831
Subtotal		**$105,421,375**
Nairobi-Thika highway improvement project (one of three segments)	2010/2011	57,053,326
	2011/2012	45,052,420
Subtotal		**$102,105,746**
Drilling of Olkaria IV geothermal wells	2010/2011	52,797,063
	2011/2012	36,041,936
Subtotal		**$88,838,999**
Kenya power and distribution system modernization project	2009/2010	7,483,545
	2010/2011	18,189,158
	2011/2012	46,178,731
Subtotal		**$71,851,434**
Kenya e-government	2009/2010	16,900,197
	2010/2011	7,275,663
	2011/2012	1,312,152
Subtotal		**$25,488,012**
Enterprise messaging and collaboration system	2011/2012	43,700,848
Rehabilitation and upgrading of equipment in universities and technical training institutes	2011/2012	27,819,870
Procurement for equipment	2009/2010	17,767,813
Kenya rural telecommunication development program	2009/2010	54,992
Total		**$483,049,089**

Source: GAO analysis of Kenyan government data.

[a]Loan commitments are shown for each Kenyan fiscal year (July–June).

U.S. and Chinese Investments in Kenya

From 2007 through 2011, cumulative U.S. foreign direct investment flows were $12 million, while China's reported foreign direct investment flows totaled about $230 million (see fig. 31). According to experts, data on China's foreign direct investments are generally underreported,[11] and according to BEA, data on U.S. foreign direct investments may be underreported,[12] limiting precise comparisons of the United States' and China's investments.

---

[11]According to experts, Chinese firms set up subsidiaries, in places such as Hong Kong and the British Virgin Islands, that can be used to make investments in sub-Saharan Africa. Such investments are not captured by China's data on foreign direct investment and may be a significant source of underreporting. In addition, many small and medium-sized enterprises may not register their foreign direct investments, which therefore may not be reflected in China's data. According to an International Monetary Fund (IMF) working paper, China's foreign direct investment data also show inconsistencies between investment flows and changes in investment stock that are difficult to explain (see Montfort Mlachila and Misa Takebe, "FDI from BRICs to LICs: Emerging Growth Driver?" *IMF Working* Paper, WP/11/178 [2011], 11). Finally, China does not define foreign direct investment when reporting its data. However, the types of data China reports for its foreign direct investments (e.g., equity investment data, reinvested earnings data) are similar to data reported for U.S. foreign direct investment. Moreover, China's reported foreign direct investment data represent official information published by the Chinese government and, despite their limitations, have been used in various reports, including those published by international organizations (e.g., the IMF), government agencies, academic experts, and other research institutions, to describe China's foreign direct investment activities in Africa.

[12]BEA noted that these data may not include investments in Sub-Saharan Africa by U.S. firms through subsidiaries in locations such as the Netherlands. According to BEA, U.S. foreign direct investment data are based on a 2009 benchmark survey that covers the value of all U.S. foreign direct investment, but these data may not reflect foreign direct investments by smaller firms.

Figure 31: Reported Flows of Foreign Direct Investment from the United States and China to Kenya, 2007-2011

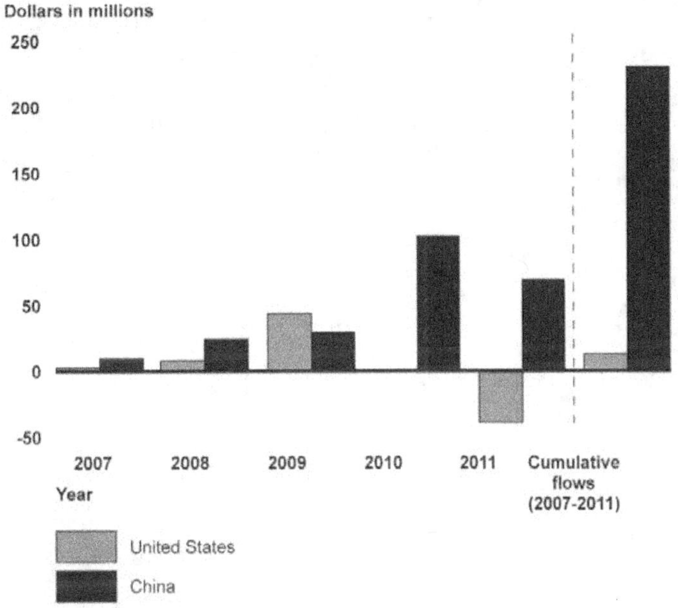

Dollars in millions

Source: GAO analysis of data from BEA, China's Ministry of Commerce, China's National Bureau of
Statistics, and Haver Analytics.
Note: Data are shown in nominal values.

From 2006 through 2011, according to BEA, the majority of U.S. foreign direct investment stock in Kenya was in finance and insurance and grew at an average annual rate of 20 percent. Growth in finance and insurance investments was primarily driven by investment in banks. Manufacturing, led by chemicals and transportation-equipment manufacturing, was the second largest sector but declined at an average annual rate of 3 percent during this period. Sectoral data for China's foreign direct investment stock in Kenya were not available.

Appendix I: GAO Contact and Staff Acknowledgments

Contact	David Gootnick, (202) 512-3149 or gootnickd@gao.gov
Staff Acknowledgments	In addition to the contact named above, Celia Thomas (Assistant Director), Fang He, Farhanaz Kermalli, and Mona Sehgal made key contributions to this report. Gezahegne Bekele, Ming Chen, Lynn Cothern, David Dornisch, Mark Dowling, Philip Farah, Etana Finkler, Bruce Kutnick, Reid Lowe, Marc Molino, Mary Moutsos, and Jeremy Sebest provided technical assistance.